The I AMs of Jesus

The I AMs of Jesus

Francis Lyall

MENTOR

Other religious books by author

Of Presbyters and Kings: Church and State in the Law of Scotland (1980)

Slaves, Citizens, Sons: Legal Metaphors in the Epistles (1984).

Published in the Mentor imprint by
Christian Focus Publications Ltd.
Geanies House, Fearn, Ross-shire,
IV20 1TW, Scotland, Great Britain.

Cover design by Donna Macleod

CONTENTS

For Fiona Elizabeth

PREFACE

The purpose of this book is to explore the series of statements about himself that Jesus makes in the Gospel of John. In each he says 'I AM'.

This book is not to be read straight through. I suggest no more than one chapter a day (and perhaps less) should be read. I also suggest that at least a day is left between chapters. The diet is rich, somewhat concise and takes time to assimilate. Go too fast and you will pay the same penalty as the gourmand. Alternatively you will be like the tourist who thinks Europe can be 'done' in a week, but is left exhausted with only a rather unhelpful blur of capital cities and some other 'important sights' (or 'sites') of a very diverse continent.

It would also be useful to read with a Bible by your side. Reading the context of each saying is important for our understanding of what is being said – what is going on, when, how and to whom Jesus was speaking – contribute to the points he is making.

How one reacts or responds to these statements is up to each individual. I would not say 'do this' or 'feel that' – that is not my vocation. Indeed, I would say that if you ask 'what then should I do?' or 'how should I respond to all this?', this book has failed. Rather, I hope that through considering these statements you make better acquaintance with Jesus himself, and if so, that sort of question will not arise.

The origins of this book lie in a sequence of Bible studies I prepared over the course of a few years for my home

church, Gilcomston South Church of Scotland, Aberdeen.
I am grateful for comment by some of the various audiences, and later by certain individuals on whom this text
has been tried out. I am particularly grateful to my minister, the Rev. William Still, whose systematic exposition of
the entire Bible has taught me much over the more than
one-third of a century that I have been a member of 'Gilc',
and for his comment on an early draft of these pages.

My trade is academic law, not theology or New Testament studies. That will be obvious to the experts in those
latter fields. The Appendices provide some information on
my sources and *modus operandi*. My own theological stance
could be described as on the Calvinistic side of C. S. Lewis,
summarised as traditional orthodoxy with some emphasis
on the sovereignty of God.

Finally, as I have written elsewhere, I would ask those
who can discern such things that they would 'remember
Baruch' (Jeremiah 45).

F. Lyall, 1996.
Faculty of Law
University of Aberdeen
Scotland, U.K.

CHAPTER 1

LEAPING LOGIC and I AM

Several times Jesus gave terse word-pictures of himself. He said he was the Bread of Life; the Light of the World; the Door of the Sheepfold, and the Good Shepherd; the Resurrection and the Life; the Way, the Truth and the Life; and, lastly, the True Vine. There is some repetition and linking between these images, for sometimes the images join together, but in each he was disclosing something fresh about himself. The purpose of this book is to consider these phrases, to distinguish the different elements in them, to ponder their apparent and their less obvious meanings, to tune in to the resonances they evoke from various scriptures of the Old Testament, and thereby to get to know Jesus better. How you respond is a matter for you.

Suppose you were to sum up the essentials about yourself, what would you say? 'I'm a teacher'? or 'I'm a housewife'? I might tell you 'I'm an academic', or 'I'm a lawyer'. But the phrases are not very informative. What do you teach, and where? Are you a new housewife, or a widow, a mother? What does 'academic' and 'lawyer' tell you? What if I were a 'lawyer academic'? How is that slightly different from my preference, which is to say I am an 'academic lawyer'?

We can play these sorts of games. But note how typical it is that we usually define ourselves in terms of our occupations. Not much is disclosed about what we are really like; we tend to focus on what we do, our jobs, whatever takes up most of our time and effort.

Suppose you were asked to sum up the salient points about someone else – would you be more graphic, and a good deal more informative? 'She's a brick' is a very English way of indicating how someone might be coping with personal disappointment, or able to help another going through deep waters. 'He's a rottweiler' tells you a lot about him. Think about your friends, and those you are less fond of, and the images will come to mind. It is that sort of picture language that we are considering in this book.

Picture language is difficult. Different people will take subtly different things from the same words. A cat-lover might be quite happy to be called a 'pussy-cat': others might not. Yet Jesus was willing to categorise himself, using the phrases the Gospels bring down to us today. Although the impact and message of the phrases have been blunted by generations of glib use, there remains a core element – a basic self-depiction by the Saviour.

Compared with those who first heard the words, we have one great advantage in thinking about the various I AM images. We can use each image to supplement or clarify areas where another is more opaque. Think of it in either of two ways, one artistic, and one very technical. The artistic I will describe here. The technical we will come to in the final chapter.

One of my treasured memories is of a few minutes in May 1964 in the Museum of Fine Art in Boston. I came in past that magnificent bronze statue that stands in a garden space in front of the main door. It is of an Indian Chief on his horse with his arms spread wide and high, his head back, and it is called, if memory serves, 'Hail to the Rising Sun'. I went past it, in at the great doorway, and found, grouped at the base of the main internal stairway, first some of Monet's sequence of paintings of the West Front of Rouen Cathedral, and then a similar sequence of a haystack in the fields. That was the first time I had seen such pictures, and their impact has lasted. I have never been back to Boston and the layout may well have changed, but the memory has been refreshed by others of the Rouen sequence now held in such places as the Metropolitan Museum of Art in New York, and in the Musée d'Orsay and the Marmottan Museum in Paris. I have also seen some of the haystack series in the d'Orsay as well as in occasional travelling exhibitions. They are wonderful.

Both series comprise a number of paintings – apparently there are thirty-one in the cathedral series – each done from approximately the same vantage point. The angle and distance to the subject are more or less the same. The change from one picture to the next is the variation of the light as the sun traverses the heavens, and as the clouds pass by. The light changes in hue, intensity and angle. Shadows come and go. Different elements of the subject attain different emphases. The very texture of the cathedral front seems to alter as the painter records the passing hours. In the other series also one learns new things about haystacks, although they always remain the same haystacks. Both sequences are a triumph of the artist's skill, his observation and technique. At the end of scrutinising even two of either sequence (though preferably several hung beside each other) you know much more about the subject than you did when you began.

It is the same with the I AMs in the Gospel of John. There is the sequence of word pictures picking out different elements. You can think of them either like Monet's pictures, and pass from one to another, not forgetting the previous as you think about each new image. Or, as we will see, you can try to combine the imagery in the way that computers now do for the remote sensing experts. In these images Jesus speaks of himself, his character and his work. Sometimes he illustrates relationships with him. The different word-pictures bring out disparate things about him, focusing on diverse elements or giving another slant to the same point. By seeking to understand his images we therefore learn about him, and of him. It may well be that we do not fully understand – that's not the purpose of these images – but at least we can *catch* what he is saying. Jesus is trying to help his hearers (and us) grasp truth. The images have a pastoral function rather than an intellectual one. His words are given to help people perceive truth, not to satisfy academic curiosity.

Of course he is using figurative language. Jesus is not saying that he actually, and in fact, 'is' something or other. He is not a loaf, or a door. He is giving us analogies and metaphors. He is saying, 'Think of me like this'. 'Think of me like that'. The figure of speech he uses is not an intellectual and rational account of the matter. It is Jesus offering a way of thinking which allows us to appreciate and accept things about him. He is not stating the mechanics of salvation in scientific terms, nor clinically depicting God's care for his people. Jesus is simply giving us graphic images which we can take to ourselves, and act upon the truths they illustrate. But, to get the most out them, it is important that we enter as far as possible into the immediate content of the words before seeking their meaning.

This should not be a strange, unaccustomed effort. Ordinary speech is full of picture language. However, precisely because we use so many images in our ordinary speech we can forget we are doing it. If I write: 'I hope this book will cast some light on Jesus' "I AM" statements,' everyone will know what I mean. But no one expects this book actually to emit light when it is opened. The figure of speech, 'casting light,' is familiar. But that very well-knownness is crucial. When we use a figure of speech, we need to be sure that both the person using the figure *and* the person to whom it is addressed will take the same meaning out of the words (see Appendix 1). If I mean one thing by my figure of speech, but you understand something different by it, the result is confusion and a breakdown of communication between us. Many quarrels and disputes start off like that, particularly in international negotiations but also in family quarrels in which something is 'taken up the wrong way'.

Be aware of this potential for difficulty. In the case of Jesus' words it means we must start where he started. We must try, so far as we may, to know what those who heard his words would have understood by them. What connections would the bald words have made? What nuances would have filled out the content of the simple phrases? What resonances and harmonics would have been triggered off by them? Jesus knew what his audience would have taken from the imagery, and he made use of that knowledge. If we can put ourselves in their position, we too will know more of what he meant and therefore get more out of his words.

It is not an easy task. Even at first sight some of the 'I AM' statements are difficult. 'I am the Resurrection and the Life' is opaque to anyone uninstructed in the Christian faith – indeed, it's not easily plumbed even after instruction. Other images appear easier to understand, but, on exploration, have depths that are not apparent at first sight.

One difficulty is that sometimes the passage containing the phrase may have a gap in its reasoning. We have not

always been given the full transcript of a conversation. In
other cases, particularly when Jesus is talking to a crowd,
he may be fielding questions from a number of people. In
both cases it is tempting to take the biblical sequence of
the words as being the complete and logical development
of a line of thought, when in fact it may not so be. Some
steps in the discussion may have been omitted from our
text. In multiple conversations, other voices may be pursuing their separate interests within a topic.

Another difficulty can be our presuppositions. We are
the end of a line whose thought patterns go back to the
Greeks and the Romans. We 'know' what is relevant and
what is irrelevant. We 'know' what is logical and what is
not. But, while there are areas of presupposition we share
with the Jews of the first century, we should realise that
they had also other notions. For us a compelling argument
or cogent answer must conform to certain limits, the limits
which for us set the bounds of rationality. We make associations between ideas, and allow ourselves to be instructed
by figurative language only within these limits. We all know
the dangers of 'arguing by analogy'.

The Jews to whom Jesus spoke worked to different
boundaries. The first-century Jew was quite prepared to
link argument by what can seem the oddest means to us.
He would draw on and associate passages and ideas from
Scripture, commentary and folk-lore, on a basis which
often seems closer to free association than to rigorous
thought. I will call this method 'leaping logic' (see Appendix 2). For example, a Jew would be quite happy to link an
idea or principle by any perceived similarity, or even by
antithesis. Diverse ideas might thus be linked through it
being possible to present them by the same analogy. A
striking modern use of this sort of thing comes in C. S.
Lewis' *Perelandra*, when the Voice points out to Ransom,

who is hesitating whether he should physically attack the demonised Weston, that the Voice also has the name Ransom. A man called Ransom should be willing to be a ransom to save a world: isn't that why he bears that name?

Again, in Jewish practice the similarity in sound of two words could carry the mind from one idea to another. Even a pun could be employed. Think of Jesus' play on the closeness of *petros* (Peter) and *petra* (rock) in Matthew 16:18, or Paul's grim carrying forward of the imagery of cutting and circumcision in Galatians 5:12. Such verbal techniques could be carried very far. The Mishnah[1] is largely arranged on the basis of such associations, and not on what a modern lawyer would consider the proper progress of conceptual analysis. Association by sounds and rhythm was often used to bring parts of the law together so to make easier the memorising that was essential to legal education in those days. These mnemonic devices also carried through into the written version of the teaching and the parallels and explications which developed it (see again Appendix 2).

We should not think of such procedures as being either completely dead, or as improper. Think of the verbal gymnastics of many modern preachers who use all sorts of associations to carry them far beyond what pure 'western' logic would permit. The Lord can and does speak through an apparently 'non-rational' association of thoughts. We should not lightly dismiss such techniques and the truths to which they can lead.

And many of us do not avoid such leaps in other areas of thought. The burgeoning genre of 'fantasy' contains examples of the sort of illuminating transition that we can find in Jesus' words. Loosen up and let the romance of imageries carry their meaning. Take an ordinary phrase

---

1. A second-century compilation of Pharisaic teaching which is our main source for the Jewish Law of Jesus' time),

from a book: 'the door opened'. There is no impact there:
something happened. But take the same concept as
expressed in a science fiction story: 'the door dilated' –
and you have a breath of deeper meaning. It is that sort of
step that Jesus expected his hearers to be willing to take if
they wanted to understand his words.

Jesus could take it for granted that many of his hearers
would, by such leaping logic, give content to and fill out
his imagery by associating it with ordinary life, and with
Old Testament notions. The whole panoply of Jewish
history, the prophets, the Temple and the sacrifices all lay
at hand to invest his simple words with meaning. He could
communicate by implied reference to all such things. Of
course, some of his statements were deliberately difficult,
as is clear, for example, from his handling of the first of
the statements we will discuss, 'I am the bread of life.' But
irrespective of that, it is also clear that he expected his
audiences to range throughout their knowledge and experience to fill out the images in which he couched his
message.

It is also clear that his expectation was not disappointed.
See how perceptive some of the comments and questions
of the Jews were in their conversations and interplay with
Jesus. Obviously they were applying associations and
content to fill out the meaning of the bald words. For
example, there is obvious insight into the meaning of 'the
bread of life'. The Jews' responses in that discussion make
it quite clear they knew exactly what Jesus meant.

At first sight that might seem curious. (I know that to
assert they knew what he was saying runs contrary to the
traditional view that the Jews were blind to Jesus'
message.) But any such feeling of strangeness (or error) is
unfair, and is caused by our unwillingness to give the Jews
any benefit of the doubt. We are accustomed to think that

the Jews opposed Jesus and hounded him to death. So they did. But we should also remember that not all the Jews were against him. Some joined him, forming a group much larger than that of his close associates, the disciples. It may have been some of these, the later-to-be-followers, who asked the perceptive questions. Again we need to remember that the others, the opposers, were often intelligent men, who, within their lights, were seeking truth as they saw it. That they were to turn so demonically against Jesus does not invalidate their insights as they sought to make up their minds about him. Some understood, and rejected. What they obviously thought of his words will help us explore their meaning.

So, in trying to get the most out of what Jesus revealed about himself in the 'I AM' statements, we will adopt something of the same associative technique, with an addition. From our position in history we can range through the New as well as the Old Testament. What Jesus said and did throughout his life, as well as other things written in the epistles, can occasionally be brought in to fuel our consideration of what Jesus said at a particular point in his ministry.

I AM

But first, we must conclude this chapter with a general point. In each of the statements to be considered Jesus says, 'I am'. The statements are formulaic: 'I am the bread of life' is a clear example.

There is one other occasion on which that formula was used, and it is to be seen (as indeed it was seen by the Jewish authorities) as something massive. For us it must undergird our consideration of all the other 'I AMs'.

The statement comes in John 8:58. The context is a
discussion with the Jews during which Jesus has made one
of the 'I am the light of the world' statements (John 8:12).
But the argument had gone on from that point. Eventually
Jesus says to his audience that those who keep his word
will not see death (John 8:51). The Pharisees pounce.
Abraham, the greatest Jew, and all the prophets, are dead.
Is Jesus therefore greater than Abraham? Is Jesus there-
fore greater than the prophets, for they also are all dead?
And, if so, then who or what does Jesus claim to be?

Jesus replies that Abraham had seen Jesus' day coming,
and had been glad about it (John 8:56). The reply produces
scorn. 'How could that be?' was the response. Had Jesus
himself seen Abraham, Jesus being a man of less than fifty
years old? Jesus replies: 'I tell you the truth, before Abraham was born, I am' (John 8:52-8, paraphrased).

This is an example of leaping logic in action. To
modern man Jesus' words appear so simple and innocuous
– at best, foolish. To the Jews of Jesus' day, however, they
were not foolishness, but a claim to deity. The argument
works like this.

At the Burning Bush Moses was commissioned by God
to lead the Children of Israel out of Egypt. He demurred
on various grounds. But once he had been persuaded
otherwise, the one question which Moses asked was this:
'When I go to them and say, the God of your father has
sent me to you. They will say "what is his name?" What
shall I reply?' It seems that 'the God of your fathers' would
not do (Exodus 3:13). God replies: 'I AM WHO I AM. Say
I AM has sent me to you' (Exodus 3:14). God goes on in
verses 15-16 to tell Moses what else to say to the Israelites,
and uses the more traditional names of 'the LORD God of
your fathers, the God of Abraham, the God of Isaac, and
the God of Jacob'. But the important statement had been

made earlier. God had revealed himself as the Self-Exist-
ent One, whose fullest name, communicating across such
a broad band as to be almost incomprehensible, is 'I AM',
'YAHWEH', 'JEHOVAH'.

Ever after that, 'I AM' (JHWH, transliterated as
Yahweh, and in the King James Version as Jehovah) was
known to the Jews as the great and holy name of God. By
tradition that name was so holy that it was not to be taken
on the lips of man. Whenever it appeared in the Scripture a
pious Jew would (and does) substitute the name God
(Elohim or Adonai) for oral delivery of the passage.

So when, in John 8:58, Jesus said to the Jews: 'Before
Abraham was born, I am', they understood him to be claiming to be God. His words immediately linked with the I
AM of the Burning Bush. It follows that, within their lights,
the Jews were justified in taking up stones to stone him
(John 8:59). Either his claim was true (a possibility which
they would not concede or consider), or it was a blasphemy
for which stoning was the lawful penalty (Leviticus 24:16).

For us, his claim is truth. Jesus is God, and in the other
'I AM' statements in John's Gospel, he permits his immediate hearers and, generations later, ourselves to know more
of his character and his concerns. In these statements he is
telling of himself, and how we are related to him. In each
statement he takes simple picture-language – a wisp of
words – and uses it to communicate. Echoes and resonances
from experience, from history and from the Testaments
make them a channel to us, and from which we can drink.
Fragments and themes, moods, harmonics and harmonies
are drawn together into major symphonic statements about
fundamental matters.

The mixture is rich, especially when we add in the Old
Testament echoes. As with rich food, a little goes a long
way. At times it is better to read a little, then think, and

then put the matter aside for a while, so that the subconscious and the emotions can get healthily involved. These, as well as (and sometimes more than) the intellect, have a part to play in appreciating what Jesus has said. If that is not done, this mental food will be rejected as surely as one's digestion reacts to an unaccustomed and unduly rich binge. Each of us needs to know our capacity. We need to take these figures slowly, allowing time to appreciate what each image is saying, and to allow it time to do its work in both mind and heart. Go too fast and you will indeed be left in the position of that tourist mentioned in the Preface: Europe cannot be 'done' in eight days. There is no way you can get to know these images and let them do their work on and in you, without taking time and thought to them.

We need, however, to be wary of the kind of thought we employ. As said above, the purpose of these images is to help us, not to provide a narrative of the mechanics of salvation or of God's care for us. We require, therefore, to think for a purpose, that of exploring the ideas and allowing their message to come through. We should not be seeking to force the images together into some sort of synthesis with each other. Occasionally they do shed light on each other, and sometimes we come across resonances of one in close connection with the resonances of another. But we are not to try to boil them together into some sort of self-consistency. Marmalade, maple syrup, honey and raspberry jam, plum jam and lime jelly are each wonderful on their own. Put them together and you get a mess, and an unappetising mess at that.

One other thing. The reactions of the audiences to each statement have something to teach us. Some reject out of hand. Others are intrigued; they are interested for a while. Others are puzzled, but persist, trying to draw out the depths of meaning in the statement. And in one case there is a glad and immediate acceptance, resulting in a flowering of faith and love which takes one's breath away. Watch the reactions – theirs, and yours.

CHAPTER 2

THE BREAD OF LIFE

'I am the bread of life' (John 6:35, 48). 'I am the living bread' (John 6:51). These subtly different statements of the same essential point are found in one of the longest of Jesus' reported discussions with the Jews. Many had been trailing Jesus because of his miracles, which down to that point had mainly consisted of healing the sick (John 6:1-21). At Passover Jesus retreated to a mountain across the Lake of Galilee, but he did not escape from the crowds. Taking pity on them, he fed the five thousand with the five barley loaves and two small fishes (John 6:3-13). Then, to avoid the inappropriate enthusiasm of some who would have made him a king by force, he withdrew alone further up into the mountains. The disciples were left to take ship for Capernaum, and Jesus later joined them by walking on the water (John 6:16-21). The people, however, were still on his track, and caught up with him at Capernaum which is on the north coast of the Lake of Galilee. There they began again to ask questions. (It would be useful at this point to read John 6:24-71, or better, the whole chapter.)

In the conversation between Jesus and the Jews we find that typical, unusual, almost crazy logic. Some of it can be explained by our not having the full transcript of all that was said. Thus it is clear that Jesus' words in John 6:41 are reported through the reaction of the audience to them, not as and when he said them. Verse 41 – 'I am the bread that came down from heaven' – summarises the ideas of verses 32-40, and what it says is implicit in verses 33 and 35, but when did he say the exact words of verse 41?

Again, consider that the episode narrated in John 6: 25-58 took place in the synagogue at Capernaum (John 6:59). It is just possible that what we are given in the text did all take place inside the building. But the whole sequence makes it more likely that some of the conversation took place outside, when the people first found Jesus (John 6:25), with the rest being said later inside the synagogue (verse 59). Indeed, it is even possible that the discussion may have taken place over one or two days, for it is not likely that the travelling of verses 17 and 24 would have taken place on the Sabbath. If either of these possibilities are what in fact happened, then clearly we have nothing like a full report to go on. The references to the bread would therefore have been made over a period of at least hours, and we do not know the connecting discussions. But we do have enough to appreciate the teaching which Jesus offers in response to probing questions.

Whatever the length of the discussion, it is clear that the Jews had been chewing over what Jesus was saying, and even arguing it out among themselves for some time. That is why John reports Jesus as saying much the same thing several times over in different words. Either different groups of Jews were involved, or they were coming back with supplementary questions. And the Jews did have to ruminate over the words and had every reason to come back for further elaboration and clarification, for the images Jesus uses are not easily appreciated fully without thought.

The 'logic' of the discussion in John 6 focuses in the notion of bread and its associations. To be accurate one should say that the discussion has its *foci* in these notions, for many elements are present. There is the notion of bread itself, and there are the associations of 'bread', the Manna of the Wilderness, the Bread of the Presence and the Bread Offering. But first, we should observe how the idea of bread is used by Jesus to bring the discussion round to the point he wishes to make.

The simple, basic element of Jesus' figure of speech is that of 'bread'. Bread was the all important main element of the local diet, much as similar flour cakes are in the Indian sub-continent today. It was not the crusted or sliced polythene-wrapped loaf from a modern western bakery or supermarket, or the fancy French bread that is so pleasant. We are talking about the basic diet of the common people in a first-century eastern land.

Because of the need for bread, the sound of the mills was a major feature of life. In any village the noise of the grindstone would be present for much of the time. It would be easily heard, there being little other sound to mask its distinctive scrunching grate. That is why Ecclesiastes 12:3 and 4 refer to the grinders being few, and the sound fading as grinding ceased. Of course, in the Ecclesiastes verses there is the poetic transfer of the image to the decay of life as one ages, and sinews, eyes and teeth go. But the imagery is based firmly on the decline of a village community, where one evidence of decline was precisely that the normal pervasive sound of the mill was absent.

Other passages bolster the point. In Jeremiah 25:10 the Lord prophesies judgement. The Lord will 'banish ... the grinding of the millstones.' The imagery is taken up also in Revelation 18:22, where the angel of the Lord throws a millstone into the sea and proclaims that 'the sound of a millstone shall never be found in [Babylon] again.' So, in

Jesus' time the absence of the sound of the millstone was a
sign of disaster. It meant that there was no more bread. No
more food was being prepared for that community. No noise
of grinding meant the end, for bread and its production
was of fundamental importance.

But why did such a topic arise in John 6? How did the
people come to ask for the bread of which Jesus spoke
(John 6:34)? How was he given the opportunity to express
himself in such intriguing terms?

The short answer is that Jesus made the opportunity for
himself. When the people asked Jesus when he had arrived
in Capernaum (perhaps with the implication that he should
have informed them, or expressing surprise he could have
travelled so far so fast), Jesus ignores their question.
Instead of answering it, he turns on them with a challenge.
They had sought him out. They had pursued him, rowing
all the way across the Sea of Galilee (John 6:24), because
he had given them bread to eat. He alleges that their interest in him was merely that of seeking food. They had not
come because of any of the miracles. Even the miraculous
feeding of the five thousand weighed with them only
because it had filled their stomachs (John 6:26).

This is an astonishing claim, because on other occasions,
and even at verse 2 of John 6 itself, we are told that miracles had drawn the crowds. But that is what Jesus says:
food was the driving force for these people. Hunger is less
satiable than an appetite for wonders. But Jesus immediately uses that fact. Quickly he takes their attention off the
miraculous and snuffs out any lingering interest in tricks
by talking to them about food. That his gambit was effective shows that his allegation was true, and bolsters my
general point that food was a much greater problem for the
average first-century dweller in the Holy Land than it is
for us today. Jesus then leads his questioners to think of

enduring food – a compelling and captivating notion in the Capernaum of that day.

It is a curious conversation. Jesus tells them that they have sought him out for food, but that they should seek everlasting food, the food which the Son of Man could provide (John 6:27). They make a classic human response. How can they get it? Jesus has spoken of working for food which endures to eternal life. He has also spoken of the Son of Man giving it. They do not, however, take up the point about gift. Their assumption is that the giving will be in response to their having earned that food. It is not too much to see in this a shadow of Romans 4:1-25. The acceptance of the gift of God through faith is not the same as earning something, doing something for which the just and equitable reward is a right to receive – a lesson we all have to learn.

But the Jews were sufficiently principled to see that not just any sort of work would do. They want to earn this eternal bread by working the work of God. So, they ask, what is the work they have to do (John 6:28)? Given what else Jesus had already said, the question seems strange; but Jesus answers it. The work of God is to believe in him whom God has sent (John 6:29). The answer therefore throws the Jews back to the answer to their first question. The Son of Man – Jesus himself and belief in him: these are the nub of the matter of the living bread.

It is important now to note that the Jews do not misunderstand Jesus' answer. Yes, they slide off the point almost immediately. But not *actually* immediately. They do see the point. They accept that he is talking about himself, not some other 'Son of Man'. Jesus has said that the Son of Man has been sealed by God, that is that he has been authenticated and given authority by God's imprint (John 6:27). So they ask him for proof. They do not ask 'Who is

this Son of Man?' They do not wall off the notion in the
way that modern intellectuals would do: 'Son of Man? What
an interesting notion!' No! Their reaction is clear and definite. Jesus is talking about himself. So, what proof can he
show that he is in fact the Son of Man that he claims to be?
'Why should we believe you? What proofs can you show?'
(John 6:30)

Only then, but then how quickly, do they slide away from
the point. It is as if they had peered over the edge of some
precipice, and then backed smartly off. Is it some other
voice in the crowd which asks the sidetracking question
that recalls their attention to the matter of evanescent physical food? Or are they just groping, harking back to the miracle of the loaves and the fishes? For now the questioners of
verses 30-31 in effect ask Jesus: 'Is there a connection between what you did yesterday feeding that crowd, and what
happened in the Exodus?'

Jesus stops only to correct any possible misunderstand-
ing that it was Moses who provided the manna (verse 32),
and gets back to his point. His Father gives true bread from
heaven. 'For the bread of God is he who comes down from
heaven and gives life to the world' (John 6:33).

Again the Jews follow what he is saying. They ask to be
given that bread (verse 34), and Jesus then explains in solemn words which are summed up in their beginning:

> 'I am the bread of life. He who comes to me will never go
> hungry, and he who believes in me will never go thirsty.
> But as I told you, you have seen me and still do not be-
> lieve' (John 6:35-36).

The rest of John 6 elaborates these points. I do not want
in this book to try to go into the massive questions of God's
choice of some which is expressed in such verses as 37, 39
and 44-45, for that would take us away from our focus. But

these points exist. Of course they exist in tension with the free offer of forgiveness in yet other passages. All I would say is that this is the profoundest mystery; two apparently incompatible truths, but truths which must be held in tension for a proper understanding of the gospel.

One other thing: remember what had so recently happened – the events that seem to have triggered the questions. The first section of John 6:1-13 is the account of the feeding of the five thousand, and that, according to Jesus, was the reason why the crowds had pursued him (John 6: 26). Surely when John was writing the rest of the chapter that sharing of miraculous bread must have provided a passacaglia for his thoughts.

Now, on to the kernel of our investigation: 'I am the bread of life.' What then did that mean to Jesus' audience? What implications are carried by such words? What do they mean to us? We can delve further into them by considering four separate referents: Bread; Manna; the Bread of the Presence (Shewbread); and lastly, the Bread or Cereal Offering. These are examples of bread in the Old Testament that were known to Jesus' audience, and which, given 'leaping logic', he could have expected most of them to have in mind as they pondered his words.

Bread

As has been said, bread was a fundamental part of life for most of the community of Jesus' time. In its various forms bread was the ordinary diet, supplemented occasionally by fish or meat. We need to remember that the diet of today is very different from that of that time. For the average person in first-century Judaea and Galilee bread was a staple,

and other foods were only an occasional treat. The modern
large-scale production of meat and fish was not practised,
and most of what was then produced was reserved for the
upper classes as of right, or ended up on their plates by
reason of their purchasing power. Those who owned the
land worked it by their hired servants and slaves, and took
the bulk of the produce. Those who could afford to buy,
bought. And there were always some who, by reason of
their political position, were 'entitled' to a higher standard
of life and diet. Only those in one or more of these catego-
ries could enjoy meat and fish on a regular basis.

For the less-favoured in the community, bread was the
staple of existence. And even that staple was not always
plentiful. Virgil's *Eclogues* and *Georgics* celebrate a gen-
erous agricultural and pastoral way of life, but that was far
removed from the exigencies of first-century Palestine. The
storerooms of Herod's fortress at Masada were full, but
that was at the expense of the ordinary folk. The only large-
scale production of grain that approached modern
intensity occurred in Egypt, from whence the corn galleys
supplied even Rome itself in a well-organised trade which
was closely supervised. The capital, Rome, was getting
accustomed to keeping its disadvantaged and unruly lower
classes happy by free bread, and the occasional circus.
Indeed, 'bread and circuses' was to become a catch-phrase:
panem et circenses. For the rest of the Empire and its
associated states, bread was the standard food, earned,
occasionally scarce through drought and crop failure, and
essential for existence.

Therefore, in calling himself the bread of life, Jesus was
identifying himself with a fundamental and essential part
of the diet of his hearers. There is, therefore, a holy fitness
(and a soaring logic) that Jesus, the bread of life, should
have been born in Bethlehem, for in Hebrew *beth* means

'house' and *lehem* means 'bread.' Our Saviour was born in
the House of Bread.

We need not throw ourselves into an artificial enthusiasm for modern bread in order to appreciate what Jesus
meant by his phrase. *Lehem* does not mean bread simply in
the sense of flour, water, salt, yeast and heat. These are
certainly included, but there is an extra element in the word
which allows it to mean sustenance in all its forms. Indeed,
the King James Version's use of the word 'meat' gives the
same sort of meaning. In Scotland you encounter it in the
'Selkirk Grace'.

> Some hae meat and canna eat
> And some would eat, but want [lack] it.
> But we hae meat, and we can eat
> And sae the Lord be thankit.

In these few traditional lines the word 'meat' does not
necessarily mean the flesh of animals. Scots 'meat' is
simply food. It might be flesh that the Lord is being thanked
for, but any fare is covered by the term. Similarly, in the
traditional form of the Lord's Prayer, the King James
Version, 'Give us this day our daily bread' does not refer
simply to loaves. To use the imagery of the feeding of the
five thousand earlier in John 6, there is no reason why the
'bread' in the Lord's Prayer should not be fish. The point
is that we thank God for the sheer basic sustenance which
he gives us, irrespective of its outward form. That Jesus is
'the bread of life' includes the meaning that he is 'the
sustenance of life'.

Something else may be taken from the Lord's Prayer.
The phrase is 'Give us this day our *daily* bread.' It appears
that the word translated as 'daily' may mean 'bread for
tomorrow', as is indicated by the Revised Standard Version variant translation of Matthew 6:11. It may also mean

'daily' in the sense of each 'today', as each 'today' succeeds its predecessor.

But there is yet another strand in the word. J. B. Phillips' translation of Matthew 6:11 follows such early writers as Origen (c.184 - c.254) in connecting the Greek word for 'daily,' not with time, but with sufficiency. In such view, prayer is made for today's bread, and for it to be given with sufficiency. Such a reading may fit better with Jesus' remarks about not being anxious for tomorrow, which are found at the end of Matthew 6:31-34. An occasional insufficiency of food, which is otherwise freely given, could be a sadistic joke.

Now, see the light which such considerations shed on Jesus as the bread of life. I would not spoil the point by over-stressing it, but do see it. In this aspect of 'bread', Jesus, as the bread of life, is the sustenance of life, given to us in sufficiency for each day.

See also how that blending of notions can illuminate the conversation with the Jews. Jesus' claim to be the bread of life comes in response to their asking him to give them that bread of God which comes down from heaven and gives life to the world (John 6:32-34). Surely there is some penetration in their asking? However, when he makes the answer plainer, they shy off (verse 41), and Jesus then deals with their unwillingness to believe in equally direct manner. They would not accept him in the way in which one must accept food.

Jesus is sufficient sustenance – he is all we need. He is the bread which comes down from heaven – that is what he told the Jews. But the thing about food is that, for it to do you any good, you have to eat it. You have to ingest before food will sustain and nourish. You have to make it part of you. There is a close parallel between the physiological and the spiritual process. We eat bread. We need to eat and digest food. Jesus is the bread of life. Food does no good in the larder or in the freezer. It does no good merely to inhale its aromas. It does no good just to chew. You have to swallow and digest. But that seems to be precisely what the people refused to do. They started to shuffle away from the directness of Jesus' words. 'Is this not Joseph's son? We know his folk. He can't be anything special' (John 6:42). With these sour words many of the people, who apparently had started to think of great and serious things, began to sidle away from the best nourishment which they could possibly have had.

The Manna

Towards the end of Chapter 1, we noted that on occasion the insights of the Jews were very perceptive. That comment was triggered by my realising that it was the Jews who introduced the matter of the 'bread from heaven'. It is they who speak of the heavenly manna in John 6:31. Jesus has only referred to 'food which endures to eternal life which the Son of Man will give you' (John 6:27). It was the Jews who made the connection between Jesus' words and manna by asking him what sign of his authority he would give. Could he produce something similar to that of the manna in the wilderness?

Whether out of mischief, curiosity or bewilderment, some in that crowd had connected the miracle of the feeding of the five thousand of the previous day by the loaves and fishes (John 6:1-13) with the question of the food that endures that Jesus speaks of in verse 27. Jesus had invited that connection in verse 26, but he seems to have tried to lead them past it to the matter of the living bread. The Jews, however, either wanted to take things more gently, step by step, or they wanted to go into matters more thoroughly, exploring every possible avenue along the way – which was characteristic of the way their minds worked.

'Wait a minute, Jesus. There was another example of food being provided for the people. What was it? The manna! All right. What connection might there be between that miraculous heavenly provided food and whatever you're talking about?'

Was the question mischievous or genuine? Probably both, for we are dealing with a crowd. Some would have been ignorant, and would not have thought through the question at all. But once it had been asked they would have wanted this new entertainer to show his prowess by coping with it. Others would have pored over the Law from their childhood and would immediately have seen a potential link between the eternal food Jesus was speaking about, the miracle food of the previous day, and the manna. It is an example of leaping logic at work. By leaping logic they would easily have passed from bread, through the bread which endures and which is to be given by the Son of Man, to the manna of Exodus 16. The Son of Man was a clear reference to someone with a special link with heaven. Eternal bread and bread given by such a Son must be bread from heaven. And 'bread from heaven' is precisely what manna is called by God himself in Exodus 16:4.

Then, as now, people were taken up with the idea of manna. It is strange that the provision of a special food for a few wandering people not otherwise known to the historical records of the time, and provided for only some forty years some forty centuries ago, should be so familiar to us. It is familiar not only to myopic Bible students, but also is a common figure of speech. As ignorance spreads with the triumph of modern education, the currency of the word is diminishing, and yet it is still familiar, usable without further explanation. Manna – heavenly provision for need.

Manna – '*Man hu?*', 'what is it?' The Hebrew of
Exodus 16:15 may be the basis of the name of verse 31,
but whether or not that is the case, it is true that the Jews
had struck on one resonance of Jesus' imagery. Manna as
bread from heaven was a gracious act of God to a people in
need. We are not told that either Moses or Aaron had prayed
for it, and it is certain that the people were not praying.
They were grumbling – a rather different activity (Exodus
16:2-3). In other places we are told when something happened as in response to a prayer of Moses, so I am inclined
to believe that, in the case of the manna, there was no prayer
at all. The people were in trouble, and in urgent need of
food, so the Lord provided the manna and quails out of his
goodness. The people were grumbling because of their need,
and God provided for the nourishment of the grumblers.
You cannot get more gracious than that!

And, apart from its origin, there is a whole stack of
curiosities about the manna and its collection and storage.
The manna was collected every day except the Sabbath
(Exodus 16:4-6). Every day that they collected, the people
gathered enough for their requirements. Whether working
hard or not, each collector had an *omer*[1] for each person
for whom he was responsible (Exodus 16: 16, 18). In some
curious way, therefore, irrespective of effort, there was an
equality of distribution according to need (Exodus 16:17-18).

On the other hand, when collecting on a Friday before
the Saturday Sabbath, each found that he had collected
enough both for that day and for the day following
(Exodus 16:22-23). That meant that they did not have to
collect food on the Sabbath, which would have been to profane it. Again the miracle of distribution was involved. On
the Friday they collected two omers for each person for

---

1. An omer was about 2 to 2.2 litres in volume, around 3.25 pounds
dry weight imperial measure.)

whom they were responsible (Exodus 16:5 and 22), and on
the Sabbath there was no manna (Exodus 16:27), as the
Lord had said (Exodus 16:26). Curiously also, while the
manna collected on ordinary weekdays was found to be
full of worms and became foul if it were kept until the
following day (Exodus 16:24), manna collected on a
Friday kept fresh for the Sabbath's needs (Exodus 16:24).

Clearly the story of the manna can shed light on the
words of John 6. The bread of life is gracious provision
made for the needs of those who will go and gather it. The
provision made is sufficient for our needs, and, in a sense,
there is equality in the provision made for each of us in
that enough is made available for each individual's needs.

But what about the equality of provision irrespective of
how hard we gather? There are two elements here. The first
is gathering for others; the second is gathering for oneself.

As to gathering for others, there is the work which is
done by anyone who studies the Word of God with the purpose of communicating it to others; gathering for them, as
it were. If he does a genuine job of work, the sermons,
writings and general life and conduct of such a person will
provide for the need of those who depend on him.

But what if he is slothful, a bad pastor and teacher who
neglects the feeding of those for whom he is responsible?
In that case I would include in the notion of providing for
need, the notion of accentuating need. It may be that the
'slothful' collector will do what God wants him to do,
almost despite himself. There are examples of such failures as ministers nonetheless having some beneficial
effect. Their shortcomings stir up some, making them
conscious that they have a need that is not fulfilled by the
ministry they are under, and they go elsewhere for that need
to be satisfied. Somehow, the 'slothful' collector performs
a preliminary function, which is to draw attention to the

fact of the unmet need. That, of course, is not to excuse the slothful – such a man will be dealt with by God for his neglect of his duty and privilege – but it affords a way to tie together the question of the manna and the slothful collector with Jesus as the bread of life.

The second question raised by the analogy of the manna is that of equality of gathering in respect of each person's own need irrespective of how hard he works. If a person works hard gathering from the Word of God for himself – or if he does not – is there the same result in an equality of provision for him? This used to puzzle me, but it is an unreal question. You cannot be fuller than full!

I wonder whether the puzzle here may simply indicate that there is for each of us a limit to the benefit of Bible study, sermons and uplifting literature. Is there not a point at which we should close the book and get out and do other things, putting into practice what has been learned, and using the 'food' we have gathered and digested, as energy? We eat to live, not live to eat. Is there such a thing as spiritual obesity?

But, of course, there is another danger to be borne in mind. Failure to gather at all could be disguised from others, and even from oneself, as 'gathering a little, but enough'. Again the practical analogy is close. If, persistently, we gather little, determinedly not wading into the riches of God's provision for us, our capacity to gather will shrink, just as your ability to eat a huge meal diminishes if you go on a low-intake diet. The stomach shrinks, and our ability to digest rich food vanishes. Our effort must therefore truly reflect our capacity, and we should know what our capacity is. And surely our capacity for Christ does increase with usage and exercise.

What about the rotten manna? That can be related both to Jesus and to the Bible. To take the latter first, if we do not read and study daily when we may, we will have only half-recollections and impressions to help us when we need it. We must keep our 'Bible manna' daily replenished and therefore fresh. As for Jesus as manna, the analogue is true. He is not a service to be called in when needed and forgotten the rest of the time. He is a friend, constantly with us if we will have it so (John 14:23). Manna could not be kept in a basket until required, except so as not to profane the Sabbath. Unused, the manna went rotten except under the special circumstances of compliance with the religious laws. It is the same with Christ. He cannot be kept in some sort of box in our hearts as an emergency ration to be taken out and consumed only in dire circumstances. At that point we will find only husks and dryness. It is the same with his Word.

Manna had one other function. It ceased to be provided the very day that the people had their first meal of the grain of Canaan (Joshua 5:12; cf. Exodus 16: 34). But one pot of manna remained for centuries in a position centrally placed in the worship of the Jews. In Exodus 16:32-34 the Lord commanded that an *omer* of manna – that one day's supply for an individual – should be put in a pot and placed before the Lord in front of the Tables of the Law, the Testimony. This was to remind the people of God's gracious provision for their physical need of food throughout the wanderings of the Exodus.

No-one knows what eventually happened to that pot of manna, any more than we know what happened to the Ark of the Testimony and the other furnishings of the Temple. It is, however, mentioned in Hebrews 9:3-5 as being placed along with Aaron's Rod and the Tables of the Commandments in a gold ark or container in the Most Holy Place. That is a measure of the importance which the pot of manna held in the religious practices of the Jews.

It seems to be that pot, in which was the hidden manna, that is referred to in Revelation 2:17. In addition to a new name written on the white stone, God will give 'he who overcomes' some of the hidden manna to eat. What does that mean? I read it. I think I know, for it rouses echoes and rings bells. But I cannot put words to what I understand by it. 'To eat of the hidden manna ...' What do you think, or feel? Is this a reference connecting to the bread of life?

It might be, for there is one other reference to manna which the jumping associational logic of the Jews should have brought to their minds. But it is a more penetrating and challenging text, which would not have been welcome just because it bears more clearly on Jesus' message. On the very banks of Jordan, Moses warned:

> Remember how the LORD your God led you all the way in the desert these forty years, to humble you and to test you in order to know what was in your heart, whether or not you would keep his commands. He humbled you, causing you to hunger and then feeding you with manna, which neither you nor your fathers had known, to teach you that man does not live by bread alone, but on every word that comes from the mouth of the LORD (Deuteronomy 8:2-3).

'Man does not live on bread alone, but on every word that comes from the mouth of the LORD.' These are the words with which Jesus rejected the temptation of the Devil in Matthew 4:4. They are also words which the crowd could have used to illumine what Jesus had said about the bread which endures in John 6:27. They are more relevant than manna to the discussion that day at Capernaum. Were they forgotten (or at least not raised), because they were uncomfortable? Were the Jews living by the words that came from the mouth of God, or had they by their rituals shielded themselves from actually recognising his words? And might that not connect with the 'bread of God ... he that comes down from God' (John 6:32-33)? And what about the later exposition of John 6:51, beginning 'I am the living bread which comes down from heaven'?

Such at least is the trace of thought that connects strictly to manna. But for us there is also the possible help of Paul's Letter to the Colossians where he speaks of hidden things. In Colossians 2:2-3 Paul writes of the mystery of God – Christ – in whom are hidden all the treasures of wisdom and knowledge. In Colossians 3:1-4, our lives are hidden with Christ in God. Put these thoughts together with the hidden manna of Revelation 2:17, and savour the result.

The Bread of the Presence (Shewbread)

Another connection which leaping logic could have made that day at Capernaum, links the bread of life and the Bread of the Presence. This connection could be made straight from the notion of bread itself, or through the pot of manna which we have just mentioned (Exodus 16:32-34; Hebrews 9:3-5), for the Shewbread was placed just beside the pot of manna in the Most Holy Place. Let us go through what is known of this bread, before trying to fit it with Jesus' teaching.

The King James Version word 'Shewbread' probably comes from Luther or from Tyndale's translation of the Hebrew text. It is not, however, very enlightening, as it is not a word often found in modern use. What is being shown? Modern translations make the answer plainer, for they replace 'Shewbread' with 'the Bread of the Presence,' or the 'continual bread'. Thus Numbers 4:7 has instructions for the spreading of a blue cloth over the Table of the Presence, and a list of all the things which were to be placed on the Table, including the 'bread which is continually there'.

The other phrase, the 'Bread of the Presence' does not mean that the Presence is in the bread, but that the bread is continually in the Presence, for the Table of the Presence was placed in front of the Holy of Holies.

The Table of the Presence was of great magnificence. The instructions for making it are in Exodus 25:23-30. Solomon made the Table of the Presence in his Temple out of gold, and he may actually have had ten tables made for the purpose, each one being used in turn (1 Kings 7:48; 1 Chronicles 28:16; 2 Chronicles 4:8, 19; 13:11; 29:18). Splendour continues in the description that Ezekiel gives of the Table of the Shewbread in his vision of the ideal Temple (Ezekiel 41:21-22).

Twelve loaves formed the Bread of the Presence. These were placed on the Table of the Presence, either in two rows or in two piles of six (Leviticus 24:4-9). They were a perpetual offering before the Lord. The number clearly represented the tribes of Israel (cf. Exodus 24:4; 28:9-12), but the bread was not an offering in the sense of a sacrifice. Rather it was a pledge of the Covenant between the Lord and his people (Leviticus 24:8). It was also a thank-offering, a token of the sustenance which God had given to his people, a part of his gift being given back to him out of gratitude.

This bread was made out of fine wheat flour (Leviticus 24:5), and was later the responsibility of the Kohathites, both to produce and to arrange in place before the Lord (1 Chronicles 9:32). The twelve loaves remained for one week on the Table before the Presence of the Lord. They were replaced every Sabbath, and the old loaves were then eaten by the Levites in the Holy Place (Leviticus 24:9; Matthew 12:4; *Mishnah*, Sukkah 5:7-8). Only in the case of David's need do we read of the Shewbread being eaten by those not of the priestly tribe (1 Samuel 21:1-6, esp. 6).

So what of this can be taken through to inform the discussion between Jesus and his questioners? The main element is clearly that of the Covenant between God and his people. Jesus is to be thought of both as being in the presence of the Lord, and as being himself a perpetual reminder of the covenant between God and man. He is now at the right hand of God, interceding for us on the ground of his compliance with the Covenant and the Law.

However, in one aspect the association of the Shewbread and the bread of life goes beyond the traditional offering. The bread of life Jesus speaks of is for all who would eat it. The consumption of that bread is not restricted to the priestly caste. Just as David and his men ate the Shewbread when in need (1 Samuel 21:1-6), so all who are in need can eat this 'bread from heaven'. We know from the rest of the New Testament that their eating makes them 'kings and priests to God' (Revelation 1:6; 5:10; 20:6, KJV), a holy priesthood (1 Peter 2:5), and a royal priesthood (1 Peter 2:9). Only 'leaping logic' will bring these ideas into a close harmony. But it has to be done, for all senses and meanings carry truth. Jesus puts the point more starkly later when he speaks of his body as being the bread to be eaten by those who will live forever (John 6:51). Then, in words which transcend the occasion, and take us straight to the Lord's Supper, he restates the point in terms of his body and his blood which are to be eaten and drunk (John 6:53-58; cf. Matthew 26:26-28; Mark 14:22-24; Luke 22:19-20, though, curiously, not in John).

The Bread or Cereal Offerings

In thinking about what Jesus meant in calling himself 'the Bread of Life,' a Jew would also remember various Old Testament sacrifices and offerings where the material of the offering was composed of bread or its components. There were a number of these, ranging from the firstfruits of Leviticus 2:14-16 (together with Leviticus 23:10,14), to the offering of a baked cake on the part of a newly anointed priest on the occasion of his entry into office (Leviticus 6:20-23). The main other passages involved are Leviticus 2:1-13; 6:14-19; 7:11-18 and Numbers 15:1-6. It is not necessary to go into each of these in detail, nor into the precise regulations for each particular offering, but some things can be drawn out as common to several of them.

First, in each case the offering involved was not insignificant. Both Leviticus 6:20 and Numbers 15:4 stipulate that the offering was to be of one tenth of an ephah of fine flour. The ephah was divided into ten omers.[2]. In those days that was a number of meals'-worth. More intriguingly, this is why we specifically noted the amount of the manna ration provided for each individual when dealing with the manna, above. These cereal offerings were by volume the exact amount of the manna that was collected for each individual's sustenance each day. These offerings therefore echo back to the gracious provision made by God for his people in their need.

Second, apart from the case of the offering by the 'new' priest (Leviticus 6:20-23), only part of the offering – a handful (Leviticus 2:2) – was burned, the rest going to the priests for them to eat, although that part of the offering was as valuable and as holy as the part sacrificed by fire (Leviticus 2:3; 6:14-18; 7:10). The priests ate any bread or cakes

---

2. See footnote 1 on page 35

allowed to them within the Holy Place itself, and they were permitted to take flour elsewhere to use it for their needs.

Third, cereal or bread offerings had to be unadulterated. In particular they had to contain no leaven (e.g. Leviticus 2:5,11; 6:16; 7:12). In the Old Testament, leaven is often a symbol of impurity, and we should note that exclusion of impurity or sin. Nothing impure or sinful can be validly offered to God. Further, in reading an instruction to sacrifice only unleavened bread we are naturally carried to the instructions for the Passover. Unleavened bread formed part of the special meal eaten on that night when the blood of the Passover lamb protected the families of Israel from the Angel of Death (Exodus 12:1-29, see verse 8). For that reason, unleavened bread was (and is) part of the Passover feast which annually recalled the deliverance from Egypt and those dreadful events (Exodus 12:39).

In contrast, salt did not pollute and was to be added to all flour or bread offerings (Leviticus 2:13). Salt was a symbol of God's covenant with his people. For us today, reading these passages with the whole Bible before us, that point must surely be linked with Jesus' instruction to be 'the salt of the earth' (Matthew 5:13).

Fourthly and finally, the bulk of the cereal or bread-offerings spoken of in Leviticus and Numbers are thank-offerings of one kind or another. The offering is made either as the result of a vow (presumably in thanks), or just out of pure gratitude to God without there being a more specific reason for it (Numbers 15:3). Indeed, the peace offering (which is interestingly translated by the New International Version as 'the fellowship offering'), was in part the offering of bread or of a flour cake in addition to an animal sacrifice (Leviticus 7:12-15; cf. Numbers 15:1-16). It appears that a bread or flour offering was required in all cases of an offering made with thanks to God.

Feed these ideas forward into Jesus' words and you see that he, the living bread, is pure, represents (is) God's covenant, and is a significant sacrifice. In a sense he is a thank-offering both for and from us. You can even see elements of the question of the consumption of the offering also present. On one hand he is wholly consumed in his role as a sacrifice to God. On the other, we do partake of him, and this is for our benefit; an idea which occurs again in his words later in John 6 about eating his body (John 6:51).

So much for the four major associations which leaping logic can make, starting from Jesus' claim to be the bread of life. With them in mind, we can now see how again and again Jesus brought his audience back to the essential point. 'I am the bread of life' (John 6:35, 48). 'I am the bread that came down from heaven' (John 6:51).

His teaching plainly (to us) relates to his coming to die on the Cross. We can see that because of our knowledge of his life and death. What the explorations of the imagery of Jesus as the bread of life show is that he was stating his role as Redeemer early on in his ministry, and potentially making it clear to those who did not know his future.

He is manna, the bread from heaven, being the gracious provision by God for our need. He, and his Word, are manna in the sense that both require regular collection and assimilation. Yet he is more than manna. Those who ate of the first manna were sustained for a time, but eventually all of them died (John 6:49). This new bread from heaven gives eternal life (John 6:50).

Jesus is also the Bread of the Presence. Seated at the right hand of God, he continually intercedes for us. He represents, nay, he is the new covenant between God and man for those who will accept it (Matthew 26:28; Mark 14:24;

Luke 22:20), and who, out of their need, consume that bread.

Though the point is plainer in the imagery of Jesus as the Lamb of God that takes away the sin of the world (John 1:29), Jesus is also an offering, with all that entails. Essential to the relationship between God and Man, he plays a crucial role in the reconstitution of a right relationship between the eternal and the human.

He is a thank-offering to the Lord God, with all the overtones brought from the bread and cereal offerings. The translation 'fellowship-offering' in the New International Version for such offerings may obscure their fundamental nature. Their function was to celebrate the peace between the offeror and God, between God and the offeror. They did not constitute that peace. The phrase 'fellowship-offering' does, however, usefully bring out the element that the offering was also to celebrate the fact of fellowship between the individual and God. Peace can simply mean the cessation of hostilities. The offering was concerned with the more active and beneficial peace of fellowship, and it is that element which we should think of as being characteristic of the relationship between ourselves and God. Fellowship is a living together in mutual regard and aid. 'No hostilities' could just mean no contact at all, and that is light-years away from the friendship which Jesus brings.

All these elements, then, require to be held in mind when thinking of the bread of life. But there is one other recurrent theme which Jesus himself returned to frequently in the passage: the necessity of eating the bread of life.

Mildly, and then starkly, he hammers home that message to the extent that it becomes off-putting. He is urgent that he must be believed in, and that not in a mere superficial belief which does not really affect the believer. Effective belief in him requires he be assimilated into the very life and being of the believer. He is so urgent on the point that in John 6:51-56 he speaks precisely of eating his flesh and drinking his blood, and cannibalism is brought to mind. Yet that urgency is also inherent within the Old Testament overtones and associations which his words have called up. Bread must be eaten for it to do any good. If it is not eaten it is wasted. We cannot be nourished by looking at bread, contemplating it, smelling it, admiring it or merely touching it. We have to eat it. We have to digest it, and allow the bread literally to become part of us. That is what happened with the bulk of the Old Testament bread called to mind by these expressions.

In most cases, then, the various breads of the Old Testament were eaten. Only the sacrificial offering at the induction of a new priest to his office was wholly burned on the altar. In the other cases a small portion was burned. The rest, though as holy as that which had been burned, was eaten by the priest. The old Shewbread was eaten by the priests after it had been replaced with the twelve new fresh loaves for the ensuing week. The manna was eaten, except for that mysterious potful.

Again and again, therefore, the bread is eaten and is literally food. That underlines, backs up and also in a curious way foreshadows Jesus' message. The bread of life, the bread of heaven which is for life eternal, has to be wholly accepted and made part of one's being. Our nourishment is contingent upon our full acceptance of him.

Yet, bound up with that truth, Jesus also exposes the other deep mystery:

All that the Father gives me will come to me, and whoever comes to me I will never drive away ... I shall lose none of all that he has given me ... No one can come to me unless the Father who sent me draws him ... Everyone who listens to the Father and learns from him comes to me ..... (John 6:37, 39, 44, 45).

It was too hard a message for many, troubling and causing grumbling even among those who at that time would have counted themselves as Jesus' followers (John 6:60-61). And even some of those did not believe (John 6:64). So, just as Jesus had predicted in the words just quoted, many went back and no longer followed him (John 6:66). Judas Iscariot was not deterred, but many were, to the extent that Jesus asked the Twelve that amazing and poignant question: 'Will ye also go away?' (John 6:67, KJV), and drew forth that golden, glowing response from Peter: 'Lord, to whom shall we go? You have the words of eternal life. We believe and know that you are the Holy One of God' (John 6:68-69). Jesus' disciples, given him by God, had penetrated the imagery of the bread of life, and, to some extent at least, had understood.

They had understood. Do I? Do you? Do we? See past the bread to the food. See past the food to the message. See through the message to the Saviour.

CHAPTER 3

THE LIGHT OF THE WORLD

Jesus as 'the light of the world' is the most frequent picture language drawn from his own words in the Gospels. Sometimes the idea is explicit as in John 8:12; 9:5 and 12:46, while at others the language is less direct, as in John 3:19 and 12:35. Of all the 'I AM' images, this is the one that burned its way furthest into John's mind, surfacing as it does in that magnificent introduction to his Gospel, echoing the very beginning of the Bible story.

Both Genesis 1:1-5 and John 1:1-9 stress light. The parallels are worth looking at before we go further.

On the face of things Genesis speaks of the creation of light and its separation from darkness, as we read later on in the chapter. In John, 'light' is severed from a solely physical referent and is made over into a metaphorical statement about the 'true Light.' In so doing, John, like a skilled symphonist recalling Jesus' self-depiction as 'the light of the world', makes the initial major statement of a theme that permeates the rest of his Gospel.

Both John and Genesis, therefore, make use of light itself, one of the commonest of all the natural phenomena. Light is essential to virtually all life, and yet we take it for granted. We assume that there will be daylight. At night we touch a switch and there is light. Go out of doors, in the cities at least, and street lights mean that you never really consider the possibility of darkness. Some areas may be a little gloomy, but one need never actually enter a darkness.

But put yourself in the back row of a crowd listening to Jesus using such phrases. How would 'I am the light of the world' strike you?

In those days, light, apart from the daily generosity of the sun, was relatively scarce. There were no generators producing mega-watt upon mega-watt of electrical power to make life comfortable and convenient. There were no batteries, no gas, no paraffin lanterns. At night only the well-off would as a matter of course have their way lit through the streets by the fitful flare of wood and hemp torches. Indoors, either the same torches or, for poorer families, smelly candles or small oil lamps gave limited illumination. No-one brings in a 'lamp to put it under a bowl or a bed, [but] to put it on a lampstand' (Mark 4:21). Jesus' words were so blindingly obvious that they were shocking to an audience in those times. Of course a lamp had to be put where it could give the most illumination. Anything else would be sheer waste. So, someone with a message has to proclaim it. Again, the importance of light, and the uncertainty of its provision by artificial means in those days is to be seen in the parable of the Wise and the Foolish Virgins (Matthew 25:1-8). The lamps had to be kept trimmed, ready and well-supplied with oil, for the arrival of important persons such as the Bridegroom.

Yes, our lives are much more comfortable than that of the first-century inhabitant of Palestine. Yet the people of that time had privileges which modern city-dwellers have forgotten. One of the few benefits of electricity strikes and network failures is that, for a short time, they give back the glories of the stars and the wonders of walking by moonlight, two of the free pleasures of creation, which itself began with light.

The first word of creation in Genesis is 'Let there be

light,' and it is that word which is taken up and added to by John from his own knowledge and experience. In the years of living with Jesus and listening to him, the imagery of Jesus as the light of the world had clearly become very precious to John. John it is who records Jesus' use of the expression 'Light of the World' and many of the other occasions when Jesus spoke in more oblique but similar terms. Indeed, John seems absorbed, not to say obsessed, by the idea of light. Of the seventy-two times that the Greek word *phos* (meaning 'light', as in our word 'phosphorescent') occurs in the New Testament, thirty-three are in John's Gospel. It therefore was natural for John, beginning his Gospel with that variant rendition of Genesis, to move from the creation of natural light to the coming of the light of the world.

But light was not just a preoccupation of John's. Entirely apart from Jesus' own description of himself, others saw him in similar terms. In Luke 2 we read of Simeon, who had been praying faithfully in the Temple for decades, looking for the coming of the Messiah. When Mary and Joseph brought the infant Jesus to the Temple to make the sacrifice proper for the firstborn child, the old man came into the Temple, and he 'took Jesus in his arms and praised God saying: "Sovereign Lord, as you have promised, now dismiss your servant in peace. For my eyes have seen your salvation, which you prepared in the sight of all people, a light for revelation to the Gentiles and for glory to your people Israel" ' (Luke 2:28-32). Simeon saw the infant Jesus as 'a light to the Gentiles'. Recall also Zechariah's prophecy over his son, John, the one who would go before the Lord to prepare the way for him (Luke 1:76). John the Baptist (as we know him) was to be the herald of the Lord who would 'give light to them that sit in darkness and in the shadow of death' (Luke 1:79, KJV). Surely both Simeon

and Zechariah are drinking from the same well, Isaiah 9:2
and 6:

> The people walking in darkness have seen a great light;
> on those living in the land of the shadow of death a light
> has dawned ... For to us a child is born, to us a son is
> given, and the government will be on his shoulders. And
> he will be called Wonderful Counsellor, Mighty God,
> Everlasting Father, Prince of Peace.

But enough of John: what does Jesus himself say?

Jesus' claim to be the light of the world is sometimes
expressed in so many words, as in John 8:12; 9:5 and 12:46.
At other times the claim is more elliptic (John 3:19; 12:35).
The first of these latter brings out clearly both the point
about the importance of light in Jesus' time, and the
impact the words would have had. John 3:16 is standard
evangelical material: 'For God so loved the world that he
gave his only begotten Son ....' But these so frequently
quoted words run on into the figures of speech we are looking at. Whoever does not believe in the Son is condemned:

> This the verdict: Light has come into the world, but men
> loved darkness instead of light because their deeds were
> evil. Everyone who does evil hates the light, and will not
> come into the light ... whoever lives by the truth comes
> into the light ... (John 3:19-21).

The context of this speech accentuates its impact. The
words are part of Jesus' discourse with Nicodemus, that
leader of the Jews who had come secretly by night to con-
fer with this new and charismatic leader (John 3:2). Consider therefore the effect of such words on someone who
has just crept along through the dark streets of Jerusalem,
ducking from shadow to shadow to ensure that he was not

recognised. How would the repeated stress on 'light' and coming 'into the light' have struck Nicodemus? And yet the impact would have been friendly; he who 'lives by the truth comes into the light.' It was to take time for Nicodemus to pluck up his courage and stand and be counted with Jesus (John 7:50; 19:39-42), but was Nicodemus not already coming to the light in John 3? Are not Jesus' words capable of the double meaning, the general statement about men, and their particular application in the case of Nicodemus?

But that general meaning of Jesus' words is what is important for us. Jesus was sent into the world for its redemption; God *did* send his only Son (John 3:16). He came not to condemn, but to save; and yet men would not have him (John 3:16-21; cf. John 12:44-50). Therein lies the mystery of evil, and the pain of its contemplation. Like many, I know persons who are nicer and kinder, who are superficially better people than some Christians whom I also know. I know some persons who are very anti-religious, yet on the face of things are better persons than I am. None of these would rail against Jesus; they are too polite for that. But in the last analysis their stance vis-a-vis Jesus is one of rejection. 'No. *I* will be my god.' They are kindly, moral, charitable, and yet they are each the centre of their own life. But that is not a stable configuration. A satellite cannot be its own primary, and we are all satellites of God whether or not we acknowledge it. They, therefore, turn away, curling away from God himself, and going on a parabola which will eventually lead to hell. It is sore to see, and yet 'shall not the judge of all the earth do right?' (Genesis 18:25). These are matters which we must on the one hand commit to God in prayer, and yet always pray about. Indeed, they are not 'matters', they are people.

But to return to the point: there are many facets and

elements to be found in Jesus' words. There are the ideas and pictures which the words carry with them on their face. There are also resonances of Old Testament matters which those familiar with the Scriptures would have, or could have brought to fill out the meaning of that strange expression, the 'light of the world'. There are the associations that leaping logic can make. We may do the same.

Light is a beacon

Light, of course, attracts attention. It is a beacon. Thus it was the burning of the Burning Bush which attracted Moses' attention and brought him to that encounter with I AM (Exodus 3:1-4). Again, as we have already mentioned, Jesus was foreseen as a beacon to the Gentiles by Isaiah (Isaiah 9:2), that prophecy being taken up by Zechariah (Luke 1:79), and Simeon (Luke 2:32). Then there was the Star which, according to the hireling prophet, Balaam, was to arise out of Jacob (Numbers 24:17). Paid to denounce the Jews, Balaam found that he could only praise them, and did so in magnificent words (Numbers 24:15-19).

Of the elements of that oracle, the Jews fixed on the prophecy of the Star, and it rang down Jewish thought. Herod the Great, though of Edomite stock, tried to convince the Jews of the legitimacy of his rule by putting a star on his coinage, thereby asserting that he fulfilled that prophecy. Was he not of the same line as Jacob? After all Jacob and Esau were brothers. That might be thought enough to ground the connection I am making.

But Herod's action goes beyond that simple connection. It is more than interesting also to note that Herod was trying to capitalise on a preoccupation with the prophecy of the Star which was resurgent just when his coins were struck. Is it not significant to find that interest in the coming of the Messiah and in a Star rising out of Jacob was current just before the Star of Bethlehem and the birth of Jesus? Herod knew the prophecy well. That may in part explain (though never excuse) the viciousness of his response to the Star of Bethlehem, the intention to kill the child, and, when that plan had been frustrated by the Magi, the Massacre of the Innocents (Matthew 2:2-18). Herod knew what was portended by the coming of a Star.

But see, we have gone from Numbers to Matthew without a tremor. And why not? The Star of Bethlehem was a beacon if ever there was one. Whatever the physical phenomena involved, and there has been much speculation, that Star was a light to call all people, even the Wise Men from the East, to the Saviour of the world. Whether the star was bright or not, it called to those who had been waiting for it.

'Bright or not?' – that may seem a strange thing to say, but it is possible that the Star was not so very prominent. The shepherds do not seem to have noticed it, and Herod had to ask about it (Matthew 2:7). There is something for us there, which connects with the manna of the previous chapter. There are some things which it takes effort to get to know, though the labour is worth it. We should not be too easily entranced by the notion of the light of the world as suddenly flashing out in an attention-demanding way. There are the other pictures of the treasure hidden in the field, and of the pearl which had to be sought out (Matthew 13:44-46). A beacon is a beacon only if you know what it is; otherwise it is only a fire.

There is another function of a beacon. We can bring out that element if we imagine that Jesus had said 'I am the lighthouse of the world'. The point lies in the words surrounding the uses of the imagery both in John 3:16-21 and in John 12:35-50. You can also see it plainly in John 9:4.

The main function of a lighthouse is warning. It has a subsidiary function of letting a ship know roughly where the
ship is, but the main purpose is to indicate danger. Jesus
warns his hearers very solemnly, and with great urgency,
that he is the light of the world and that the alternative to
his light is darkness. The time was short. He himself will
not condemn, but whoever fails to choose him is condemned
by that failure to accept the words he has spoken.

The choice is presented and made, irrevocably. The urgency with which Jesus speaks is present in John 3, and
accentuated in John 12. By that late stage of his ministry
he had already made his entry to Jerusalem, and the Cross
was looming in the near future. Choose light, or condemnation. It is so stark for us reading centuries later. These
words must have had a poignancy for Jesus at the time, as
he knew his words were dividing his audience, depending
on how individuals chose. We need to share that attitude.
These are solemn sayings. They are not to be seized on so
as to point them with relish at others. Rather they contain
that question to which each must answer responsively or
dismissively, for in this each stands alone. We choose the
light or the dark.

Pillar of Fire

If we choose the light then other elements of the light of
the world are seen. I have just noted that a secondary function of a lighthouse is to indicate to a ship where it is, and
for us the light of the world plays such a role. If we watch
that light we know roughly where we are on the ocean of
life. But it is in the Old Testament that we find a light as a
guide, providing a far more accurate guidance system: the
pillar of fire.

The pillar, in both its forms, as a pillar of cloud by day

and a pillar of fire by night, acted as a guide to the people, and as a protection for them. Its purpose was specifically to lead the people on their way out of Egypt (Exodus 13:18, 20-22) – we will come to that. But the pillar also acted as a defence for the people as it moved round the straggling mob and came between the Israelites and the pursuing Egyptian army, and thus protected them while they made their way through the Red Sea (Exodus 13:19-20). Jesus is a protector in a similar way.

The pillar was also the guide, leading the people on, and stopping each night and at other times for a period of encampment. It was the guide for forty years. Indeed, we could go a little further in considering the pillar of fire. The common understanding is that the pillar went before the people as their guide, in the form of the pillar of cloud, and that is true. We therefore tend to think that the pillar of fire was more static, for the people were normally camped at night, when the pillar took that form. But Exodus 13:21 makes it clear that on occasion the Israelites travelled by night as well as by day. What they had to do was to follow the pillar when it lifted from its place. And when they travelled at the command of the pillar by night it not only guided and protected them, it also illuminated the actual path in which they had to tread.

This is very reminiscent of Jesus as 'the way', which we will discuss in Chapter 6. But apart from that, important echo though it is, Jesus himself said: 'Whoever follows me will never walk in darkness, but will have the light of life' (John 8:12). He does not persist in the point because the Pharisees immediately attack on the technicality of Jesus being a witness to himself, but the point is made. He is the guide and guiding light for his followers, even as the pillar of fire was light for those on the march from Egypt.

There is an ancillary point also which we should notice.

The pillar was with the people all through their wanderings, up to very borders of Canaan on a direct route and
then round and round in the desert until the faithless gen-
eration had all died, with the exception of Joshua, the son
of Nun, and Caleb, the son of Jephunneh (Numbers 14:21-
24).

But what was the pillar? Was it an angel? It may have
been for some of the time, though there is a distinction
made between the Angel of the LORD and the pillar in Exodus
14:19, and the Lord is said to have led in the pillar (Exodus
13:21-22). However in Exodus 14:24 we read that it was
the Lord himself who looked down from the pillar and then
overthrew the Egyptians in the midst of the sea. For most
purposes in the Old Testament it is not profitable to distinguish between God and the Angel of the LORD. Whatever
the truth of the matter, either as the cloud or as the fire,
their God was present with the people all of the way.

How little excuse that leaves for that complaining and
disobedient people. Their God's presence was more manifest with them than has ever been allowed to any others
before or since. Later there was the cloud resting on the
tabernacle 'in the sight of all the house of Israel during all
their travels', and lifting when they were to move (Exodus
40:38), and yet we have the story of all their failures particularly in Leviticus and in Numbers. But we should not
be too scathing in our condemnation. Christians have the
indwelling Holy Spirit. They have God the Father and God
the Son abiding within them (John 14:23). And yet how
often we forget and behave as though it were not so. We
should learn better.

Light is also glory

The Burning Bush and the pillar of fire were certainly magnificent. On an even grander scale there is the fire and smoke of Jehovah's appearance on Mount Sinai, when flashes of lightning made his presence known (Exodus 16-19). The glory of God seemed to the Israelites like a 'consuming fire when Moses went up to receive the tablets with the Law and the commands on the top of the mountain' (Exodus 24:17). Later there is the cloud descending to cover the Tent of Meeting when Moses had completed the construction of the Tent. Then the glory of the Lord filled the Tabernacle and Moses could not enter the Tent for the cloud and for the glory (Exodus 40:34-35).

Only one other time did something similar happen, and it was on a parallel occasion. At the consecration of Solomon's Temple, as soon as the priests had put the contents of the Holy Place in order, and before the official ceremonies began, the glory of the Lord descended on the Holy Place, and the priests were driven out by it (1 Kings 8:10-11; 2 Chronicles 5:13-14).

Mention of the contents of the Holy Place takes us to another connection with 'the light of the world.' The instructions regarding the contents of the Holy Place, given in Exodus 25, include specifications for the golden candlestick or lampstand. It had three branches at either side of the central column (Exodus 25:31-39; Exodus 37:17-24 narrates its making), and must have looked like the well-known Israeli emblem of today. The seven lamps of the lampstand were to light the space in front of the Tabernacle (Exodus 25:37), which meant that the lampstand would have lit both the Ark of the Covenant and the Table on which the Bread of the Presence was placed (Exodus 25:10-30; cf. the discussion of the latter in Chapter 2 above).

How far one can go in tracing out parallels between the

lampstand and Jesus' imagery is a difficult question. But we must make a connection between the lampstand of the ancient Tabernacle and that shown to Zechariah which was fed by oil flowing directly from two olive trees (Zechariah 4:1-14). Oil is a symbol of the Holy Spirit, and the prophet was told that the olive trees were the two anointed ones who serve the Lord of all the earth (Zechariah 4:14), while the seven lamps of the lampstand are the eyes of the Lord ranging throughout the earth (Zechariah 4:10). In that instance therefore God himself was intimately connected with the lampstand, just as we are told he was intimately connected with the pillar of fire (Exodus 13:24).

So we see the Lord himself in all sorts of lights in these connections: the lampstand ever burning before the Ark containing the Tables of the Law, the light glancing off the polished gold of the Mercy Seat above the Ark, and illuminating the Table with the Bread of the Presence. This lampstand therefore speaks to us of the glory of the Lord in justice, mercy and provision for his people.

But that notion of glory must lead us yet further into the Scriptures. That unfortunately obsolescent word 'effulgence' provides us with elements of what we now seek, for its Latin origins mean 'flashing out' (*e-fulgere*: e = out, fulgere = to flash), the word being used often of lightning. The word 'lightning' carries such notions as well. Glory, effulgence, lightning: these lead past the instances of the phenomena of Sinai and the other occasions we spoke of above, to the glories evidenced in persons as the Lord or his Angel showed himself to certain favoured prophets.

There is Daniel's vision of the Ancient of Days: 'His clothing was white as snow; the hair of his head was white like wool. His throne was flaming with fire, and its wheels were all ablaze. A river of fire was flowing, coming out from before him' (Daniel 7:9).

There is Ezekiel's vision in the first chapter of his prophecy. It is suffused with light, beginning with the windstorm from the north bringing 'an immense cloud with flashing lightning and surrounded by brilliant light' (Ezekiel 1:4), and going on to the description of the cherubim (Ezekiel 1:15-25). Then from verse 26 on there is the account of the throne in heaven with the likeness of a human form sitting on it.

> I saw that from what appeared to be his waist up he looked like glowing metal, as if full of fire, and that from there down he looked like fire; and brilliant light surrounded him. Like the appearance of a rainbow in the clouds on a rainy day, so was the radiance around him. This was the appearance of the glory of the LORD (Ezekiel 1:27-28).

Can we be surprised that Ezekiel fell flat on his face? Or can we be surprised at Isaiah's response to seeing the Lord 'high and lifted up and his train filled the Temple' (Isaiah 6:1, KJV)?

The 'light of the world' therefore carries formidable associations. Small wonder that, when that Light had gone back to his Father, and from there confronted Saul on the Damascus road, Saul was blinded (Acts 9:1-19; cf. Acts 22:1-21; 26:12-18), if only temporarily, and it is surely gracious that later the man, now Paul, was sent help and sight by that same glorious Lord (Acts 9:10-19).

So far we have considered instances of the glory of God or of the risen Jesus, but we should remember that holiness itself can have a glorifying effect on the human frame. After he had been those forty days in the presence of God receiving the tablets of the Law and all the other instructions given on Sinai, Moses' face shone (Exodus 34:29-35). According to Paul, Moses veiled his face so that the people should not see that glory fade (2 Corinthians 3:13), but that detail is not in Exodus. There we are simply told that the people were terrified of his shining face (Exodus 34:30), and that Moses wore the veil, taking it off to go in to the presence of the Lord, speaking face to face with the Lord (Numbers 12:8) and donning it again each time after he had told the people what the Lord had said. Moses did not veil his face when speaking to the people of the things of the Lord – which raises for us the question whether we are prone to diminish the glory which has come through learning of God.

Be that as it may, it remains true that in my experience those who walk closest with God have an inner radiance, which just occasionally 'lights up' a little bit more than the adjective 'inner' would indicate. Yes, there are problems in my saying that. And yes, I am aware that the Devil can transform himself into an angel of light (2 Corinthians 11:14): C. S. Lewis reminds us that trick is ordinary drill for the demons. But it is true; some have that inner radiance that others can detect.

Of course, 'glory' showing through a human frame reached its highest with the Transfiguration of Jesus himself. For a few moments the true glory of the Son was allowed to be seen. Jesus took Peter, James and John up the mountain and there 'he was transfigured before them. His face shone like the sun, and his clothes became as white as the light' (Matthew 17:1-8; Mark 9:2-13; Luke 9:28-36). (Why does John, with all his interest in the light of the world, and who was present on the occasion, not give an account of this? Was it just too overwhelming for him? Maybe it was too precious, or of too much personal significance.) There, for a few minutes the Light of the World was properly displayed, and the favoured three were astonished. Then Elijah and Moses appeared, and another bright cloud overshadowed them. That was too much for the disciples, and they fell on their faces, terrified. No wonder!

Taking these thoughts together, as the 'Light of the World' we can therefore see Jesus as our guide, both as to general direction and as illumination for specific steps. We can see him as our protector, and most of all we can see his glory. Of these elements it is a question how much would have been apparent to the various audiences to whom he spoke the phrase. The connections with the pillar of fire seem obvious, and those with the lampstand are no less so to those for whom the symbology of the furnishings of the Holy Place were important.

But most of all I feel that the element of glory was perhaps the most important and the most challenging. Looking at a blazing light source it is difficult to make out its features. We look through a filter of heavily darkened glass at an eclipse because the phenomenon cannot be seen by the naked eye. Even so the phraseology of 'the light of the world' may have been too dazzling for most of the people – and yet there is Nicodemus and all the others who did see enough to choose that light.

So we are back at Jesus' urgency as he said those words. Choose light. He will not condemn, but the alternative to light is darkness. By choosing him we know that we are by the act of God 'qualified to share in the inheritance of the saints in the kingdom of light'. For he has rescued us 'from the dominion [the word means "ownership"] of darkness' (Colossians 1:12-13). As 'sons of the light and sons of the day' we are to behave as such and not as if of other parentage (1 Thessalonians 5:5; cf. verses 6-10). We are a 'chosen people, a royal priesthood, a holy nation, a people belonging to God, that [we] may declare the praises of him who called [us] out of darkness into his wonderful light' (1 Peter 2:9). Our salvation is nearer now than when we first believed. The night is nearly over; the day is almost here.

So let us put aside the deeds of darkness and put on the armour of light. Let us behave decently, as in the daytime ...' (Romans 13:11-13).

Such a choice is not self-serving, although it is of obvious benefit. It is a response of love to what Jesus has done for us. That also is clear from the passages in John 3 and John 12. That love will also show itself in a love for others, which, by the grace of God, he will use to win yet others to himself. We do not become transparent in his light, but we may become translucent and in measure transfigured. His light can shine through each of us, and be refracted by our personality to others. We, as it were, can be the filter through which he can be seen. But the filter must be clean for accurate transmission to occur. It brings to mind Jesus's words in the Beatitudes, which take all that has been said as to light in this chapter and turns it full force onto us:

> You are the light of the world. A city on a hill cannot be hidden. Neither do people light a lamp and put it under a bowl. Instead they put it on its stand, and it gives light to everyone in the house. In the same way, let your light shine before men, that they may see your good deeds and praise your Father in heaven (Matthew 5:14-16).

We each need to review how we shape up to that analogy. What sort of light are you showing? Is your city attractive, or dilapidated? Or is it a well-known tourist trap?

It is also important to notice what these verses from Matthew actually say. We *are* the light of the world. Not we 'can be' or 'ought to be'. It happens irrespective of whether we are a guttering candle or an arc light: our responsibility is to shine, and let God worry about its effect. We are to let our light shine. Letting is a passive word. The passage does not say that we are to organise spectacles to show off our laser equipment, or to vie with one another in coruscation. It does not say 'witness', 'give testimony' or any of the cult phrases. It says 'let ... shine' and talks of good works.

Such a life is quiet, undemonstrative and unorchestrated. Even making all due allowance for cultural differences, the hullabaloo of much modern evangelism sickens many. The camera pans back unplannedly, the director does not cue in another camera swiftly enough, and you see the circling arms of the stewards prompting the audience to applause. The choir clips in.

No. Jesus talks of a quietness, as light itself is quiet. It is a glow, not a flash, and a glow at which others are encouraged to warm themselves. This is the Light of the World manifest within the individual, drawing others to himself. His light shines in the world through us, to the extent that we allow it to shine. In that shining, being is more important than doing. Doing of itself can be counterfeit, a going through the motions of a consecrated life while lacking the real roots of such. Consider Sinclair Lewis' *Elmer Gantry*. The only way is first and foremost to *be*, and to be in the light, letting the Light of the World into every nook and cranny of the personality. Only then can being safely issue in doing, and that only at his direction.

Finally, the Light of the World shines through the individual, but not to result in a schismatic individualism. We are talking of light, but it is the light and glow of comfort, and sometimes the all-consuming blaze. At the end of time all works will be tried by fire, and the dross purged away (1 Corinthians 3:11-13), and it may be better to get some of that purifying done early. But in general it is a matter of that light and glow of comfort, as it were of a coal fire. You cannot make a coal fire out of single, solitary lumps (unless you break them). The coals brought together and lit, somehow seem to encourage each other into flame.

So at the end of this chapter, hold together these two pictures; the Light of the World himself, and the churches (the Church?) ablaze with his fire and calling others in to comfort and usefulness.

God is light; in him there is no darkness at all. If we claim to have fellowship with him yet walk in the darkness, we lie and do not live by the truth. But if we walk in the light, as he is in the light, we have fellowship with one another ... (1 John 1:5-7).

CHAPTER 4

THE GOOD SHEPHERD AND THE DOOR

We need John chapters 9 and 10 down to verse 30 as the material for this chapter.

The imagery of the Good Shepherd has filtered its way into common, if diminishing, currency. The Good Shepherd, with the allied tale of the Lost Sheep (Luke 15:1-7), drifts around among the flotsam and jetsam of the mind. The story is a launching pad for many evangelistic exhortations and appeals, and that is fair enough. But if we want to see what Jesus was really saying about himself in using these ideas, we need to keep their precise context and content in mind.

Context

The context of the teaching is a comprehensive attack by Jesus on the Pharisees and church leaders of his day. Jesus draws a brutal contrast between how they ought to have behaved – as good shepherds – and their actual treatment of someone for whom they should have cared as a stricken lamb. We usually, however, pass over this aspect of the matter in silence as we hurry on to the familiar concepts of the Good Shepherd. But we can gain much from understanding the occasion on which the words were spoken. The story of the triggering of Jesus' imagery is in John 9.

There was a man born blind. The disciples asked Jesus whether the fault of the man or his parents had resulted in this dreadful punishment. 'Neither', said Jesus. 'He was made like that so that the power of God can be shown in him.' And Jesus made a clay poultice with his spittle and put it on the man's eyes, and told him to go and wash in the Pool of Siloam. The man did so, and came back seeing – and, not unnaturally, rejoicing (John 9:1-7). It is an intriguing story, and, given our previous chapter, we should also note in passing the reference to the light of the world and impending night in verses 4-5. We should also note, for it will be of importance in the next chapter, that Jesus specifically stated that the man's blindness was not a punishment for sin, but happened so that the work of God might be displayed in him (John 9:2-3).

When he could see, the man went back to his home, but at first his neighbours did not recognise him. Then they quizzed him about what had happened and took him to the Pharisees (John 9:8-13). True to their preoccupations, the Pharisees were more interested in Jesus' possible breach of the Sabbath than in the healed man himself (John 9:14-16). They were not happy for him. They did not rejoice with him in his new-found sight. On the contrary, they interrogated both the man and his parents for their own purposes (John 9:13-34), and the man confounded them by his replies.

To paraphrase: the man said he had been cured by a prophet (verse 18). The Pharisees, who had already made up their mind about Jesus (verse 22), said that was impossible, for Jesus must be a sinner (verse 24). Further, the cured man must be a biased witness, maybe even a disciple of this Jesus (verse 28). The Pharisees had no idea where Jesus came from or anything about him, but God had spoken to Moses and they followed Moses (verse 29).

The man countered: 'Remarkable! I agree God does not listen to sinners, but only to the godly man. But that man Jesus opened my eyes. Nobody can do that. If my curer were not of God, he could do nothing' (John 9:30-33, paraphrased).

The response of the Pharisees was immediate, and furious. '"You were steeped in sin at birth: how dare you lecture us!" And they threw him out' (John 9:34). How familiar. That is the response of many scholars when an untutored outsider dares to argue effectively with them on what they are pleased to consider to be their own ground.

The Pharisees threw the man out. But Jesus, whom he had never seen, heard about it and went looking for him. Gently he asked the man whether he believed in the Son of Man, and in reply was asked who that might be so that the man might believe in him. Jesus said, 'You have now seen him; in fact, he is the one speaking with you.' Then the man said, 'Lord, I believe,' and he worshipped him (John 9:35-38). The immediacy of the man's response and its depth are striking. Truly as Jesus had said in John 9:3, this man was born so that the works of God might be shown in him.

All this, however, did not take place in private between the two. There were others present. Jesus goes on to make a comment about blindness and judgment, the two going together, and observes that many that are blind will see and many that see will become blind (John 9:39). That provokes some Pharisees present to ask whether he is implying that they were blind, and Jesus turns on them. Because they claim to see, their guilt remains. For, although they claim to see, they had rejected the blind man, now healed, the very kind of person who, blind, should have been as a sheep to them to be cared for by them as shepherds. That is the burden of the succeeding verses.

It is to these Pharisees, therefore, that Jesus then speaks in the imagery of the Door and of the Good Shepherd. The whole passage of John 10:1-18 is an indictment of them as the self-appointed and self-proclaimed shepherds of the flock of God. We will come back to the text shortly, but it is good first to note that not all the Pharisees rejected the severe words that Jesus used. After he spoke, there was dissension among the Pharisees, some of which centred on the matter of the shepherd laying down his life for the sheep (John 10:17-18). Some thought Jesus was raving mad or demon-possessed. 'But others said, "These are not the words of a man possessed by a demon. Can a demon open the eyes of the blind?"' (John 10:21). Obviously the dissension continued for some time, for Jesus repeats the imagery while walking in Solomon's Colonnade in the Temple area at the time of the Feast of Dedication (John 10:22). Clearly he was picking up an analogy he knew had been argued amongst his audience. That is plain since he most clearly and precisely repeats the language of the sheep and the shepherd (John 10:25-30). The Pharisees do not believe, Jesus says, but his sheep do listen to his voice and follow him. Yet I cannot help wondering whether that statement is absolute and exclusive of the Pharisees. Does John 10:21 not indicate that some among the Pharisees were hearing his voice? We will find out in heaven.

Content

Now, what about the content?

The imagery Jesus uses is of the sheepfold with its door, and of the shepherd. It is given twice, for Jesus repeated the picture with variation, perhaps because the first version was not completely understood. For us, given centuries of preaching, given Sunday Schools, and that general debris of memory, there may not be too great a problem in getting a message out of the text. But that must raise two questions. First, if we can get a message out, why were the Pharisees so slow or obtuse? Second, would we and they get the same message out of the words? If not, surely we have got the wrong message, for the words were directed to the Pharisees, and their meaning must be what the words were meant to mean to them.

We can answer both these questions by asking a third question: what could the Pharisees have seen in the imagery? By exploring that, we can scrape away the incrustations of Victorian tradition, and see what Jesus was saying about himself. Certainly there were many referents both in life at the time Jesus spoke, and in the Scriptures, which would have filled his imagery with meaning. He could take it for granted that his audience would make these connections and construe his words in the light of these associations.

If you add in the concepts of ram and lamb, there are over five hundred references to sheep in the Bible, most of them in the Old Testament. This is not a study of 'sheep', but do for a moment think of the Passover Lamb (Exodus 12:5) and the various sheep sacrifices. A sheep might be sacrificed as a burnt offering (Leviticus 1:10), as a sin offering (Leviticus 4:32), as a guilt offering (Leviticus 5:15), or as a peace offering (Leviticus 22:21). The lamb and the sheep analogues therefore fill to overflowing the words of John the Baptist: 'Behold the Lamb of God who takes away the sin of the world' (John 1:29). While that takes us a little away from the Pharisees, its basis does remind us of the Old Testament connotations of any reference to shepherd and sheep.

At the very least, any Jew spoken to in the obviously figurative language of a 'shepherd' would have thought of

David, taken from herding his father's flock and anointed by Samuel to be the king in place of Saul (1 Samuel 16:1-13; Psalm 78:70-72). Then again there was Moses, who spent forty years as a shepherd tending the flocks of his father-in-law Jethro before being called by the Burning Bush and commissioned to lead the people out of Egypt (Exodus 2:11-25; 3:1-2; Acts 7:27-32). For both Moses and David the skills of shepherding were to be very relevant in their leading the people. Indeed, the parallel in the case of Moses is both ironic and amusing. The shepherd who worked for forty years in the far side of the desert and the depths of Midian, was thus trained to lead a rather different herd for forty years through much the same sort of country. He was to encounter the same need to search for water, and the same recalcitrance on the part of those led – or do I do sheep an injustice?

The Pharisees, knowledgeable in the Scriptures, would also have had to reckon with direct Old Testament references to flocks and shepherds. Thus there are a goodly number of verses in the Psalms where the people are seen as a flock under the care of a shepherd, or where an individual is spoken of in that metaphoric way. A well-known example of these metaphors is the twenty-third Psalm: 'The LORD is my shepherd, I shall not want ...' Again Asaph cries, 'Hear us, O Shepherd of Israel, you who lead Joseph like a flock' (Psalm 80:1). Three times at least in the Psalms the people are said to be the flock of the Lord's pasture (Psalms 79:13; 95:7; 100:3). Jeremiah weeps because 'the LORD's flock will be taken captive' (Jeremiah 13:17), but Isaiah knows that when the Lord comes he 'will tend his flock like a shepherd, gathering the lambs in his arms and carrying them close to his heart. He will gently lead those that have young' (Isaiah 20:11). Micah prays to the Lord to 'Shepherd your people with your staff, the flock of your inheritance ... in fertile pasture lands' (Micah 7:14). Zechariah knows that 'The LORD Almighty will care for his flock' (Zechariah 10:3). Why is there such certainty? At the command of the Lord, Ezekiel repeats what the Psalmists had said long years before: 'You my sheep, the sheep of my pasture, are my people, and I am your God, declares the Sovereign LORD' (Ezekiel 34:31).

That the Lord would come and take over the care of his flock was also expressed in several passages in the Old Testament where Messiah is seen as the shepherd of his people. It may seem strange, however, to those reading modern translations that in many of these instances the language is in the plural. Nonetheless the scholars tell us that such verses as Jeremiah 3:15 were given a Messianic interpretation: 'I will give you shepherds after my own heart, who will lead you with knowledge and understanding.' Or again: 'I will place shepherds over them who will tend them, and they will no longer be afraid or terrified, nor will any be missing' (Jeremiah 23:4). That this latter verse immediately precedes the promise of the righteous Branch which was to come from the stump of Jesse (Jeremiah 23:5-6), lends justification to the interpretation of such verses as applying to Messiah. Other justification is found by taking into account such verses as Ezekiel 34:23: 'I will place over them one shepherd, my servant David, and he will tend them; he will tend them and be their shepherd.' Similar language is found in Ezekiel 37:24: 'My servant David will be king over them, and they will all have one shepherd.'

There is one curious sidelight to be seen here. Although there are these references to Messiah as 'my servant David,' there is only one reference in the Old Testament to a currently reigning king as being the shepherd of his people, and that is not to any of the godly (or even the ungodly) kings of the Jews. The reference is to Cyrus, the king of

Persia, whom the Lord speaks of as 'my shepherd' in Isaiah
44:28. There are reasons for this apparent peculiarity. It
was common for pagan monarchs to be called the shepherds of their peoples in their own chronicles and histo-
ries. However, Jewish writers avoided that particular phrase.
It is true that David 'tended' the people and that they were
spoken of as his flock, but the actual title 'shepherd' was
avoided, at least in the writing which has come down to us.
The function of shepherding was attributed, but the actual
title of shepherd was not (cf. Psalm 78:70-2; 2 Samuel 5:2;
24:17; 1 Chronicles 11:2; 21:17).

There were two reasons for this. First, as we have seen,
God himself was thought of and spoken of as the shepherd
of Israel. It would not have been right to give someone else
his title. Second, and perhaps accentuated by the association of the title with God, the human kings were really all
such failures. They did some of the job of shepherding, but
they could not truly be called proper shepherds of the people. Therefore, according to the Scriptures, only God is
spoken of as 'the shepherd' of his people in a ruling, kingly
sense, and the under-shepherd category was filled, not by
the kings but by the religious leaders, with Messiah seen
as the great shepherd who was to come.

Now it might have been thought that some at least of
these various uses of the imagery of flocks and shepherds
would have provided a content for Jesus' words in John
10, a content which the Pharisees would have read in to his
words. These men were learned. They had committed to
memory vast chunks of the Old Testament, and screeds of
the commentaries of their forebears on it. They spent their
lives arguing over the meaning of the texts, and the rabbinic traditions about it. It therefore follows that the Pharisees, with their great interest in religious matters and in
the Messiah, might well have linked the shepherd Messiah

with someone who claimed to be the Good Shepherd. But did they make these connections with Jesus' images? It seems that few did, and the reason may lie in one set of the shepherd images which they would have been reluctant to bring to mind.

False Shepherds

We have already mentioned Ezekiel's repetition of the Psalmists' description of the people as the flock of the Lord in Ezekiel 34:31, but that verse comes at the end of a chapter in which the Lord excoriates the shepherds he had sent among the flock for their neglect of their duty. Ezekiel 34 tells how the religious leaders, with the honourable exception of the occasional prophet, had fattened themselves on the very flock they were supposed to care for. For that, the Lord will come and deal with them, and will himself take over the immediate care of his people. The shepherds had exploited those in their care shamefully and ruthlessly, but an end of that would come.

A similar message is contained in Jeremiah 23:1-40, which begins: 'Woe to the shepherds who are destroying and scattering the sheep of my pasture!' It is also to be found in the ghastly images of Zechariah 11 where in the initial verses the flock is marked down for slaughter, and there is the weird foresight of thirty pieces of silver and their being cast down in the house of the Lord and given to the potter (Zechariah 11:12-13; cf. Matthew 26:14-16; 27:3-10). The diatribe continues through chapter 12 though without the use of the language of sheep and shepherd, and then into chapter 13 where the sheep and shepherd language recurs. At verse 7 of chapter 13 the prophet breaks out, 'Awake, O sword, against my shepherd, against the man who is close to me .... Strike the shepherd and the sheep

will be scattered' (Zechariah 13:7). 'Strike the shepherd ...
scatter the sheep': these words were quoted by Jesus himself just before Gethsemane as he explained to the disciples that they too would run away (Matthew 26:31; Mark
14:27). But even without that reference these words have a
dread mysteriousness as we contemplate history, even re-
cent history and the names of Babi Yar, Auschwitz-
Birkenau, Dachau, Treblinka, Stuthoff, Maidanek,
Chelmno, Sobibor and Belsen toll in our ears. Prophecies
can have a multiple application.

But at the time that Jesus spoke, the words of Zechariah
and the others were surely of relevance. Did they not explain the Maccabean wars, and the occupation of the Land
by a greater adversary, Rome? And yet it seems that there
was an unwillingness to apply these prophecies to their
most obvious target of the day, the ruling ecclesiastics of
the time. That is clearly seen in an attitude to shepherds
which was extraordinary to the point of psychosis.

In the Judaism of Jesus' time there was a considerable
concentration on the metaphoric notion of 'shepherd.'
Moses and David were routinely praised as having been
true shepherds, since they were leaders and teachers of the
Law. The Guardian of the Camp of the Essenes, that curious sect of the time, was required to treat those under his
care as a shepherd does his sheep.[1] The metaphoric shepherd was therefore seen as someone of high standing, being associated with noble and eminent figures of the past.

But, simultaneous with such praise of the metaphoric
shepherd, the status of the actual shepherds of Jesus' day
was depreciated and devalued. A nation, whose history
began with the nomadic herds of Abraham, Isaac and Jacob,

---

1. See *The Damascus Rule*, CD XIII, 9-10: See Geza Vermes, *The
Dead Sea Scrolls in English*, 3rd. ed. JSOT Press, Penguin Books,
1987, pages 10 and 97).

and for whom the former shepherds, Moses and David, were heroes, was latterly taught to condemn shepherding as an occupation. Doubtless the economy was in a mess, and doubtless the shepherds were suspected, often justifiably, of making sure that they were all right. But even if one gives the maximum play to such excuses, they do not explain the extent to which the occupation was downgraded. Civic privileges, including those of being either a judge or a witness, were withdrawn from shepherds. The other class similarly to lose its privileges was that of the tax-collectors – an intriguing parallel, for the Gospels make plain the extent to which those were despised as collaborators with Rome, quislings. The rabbinic midrash (commentary) on Psalm 23 says: 'No position in the world is as hated as that of shepherd.'

Why? When I first read of how a respectable calling had so declined in public esteem it was shortly after reading all those dreadful prophecies and the severe criticism in Ezekiel, Jeremiah and Zechariah. The immediate thought was quite unprovable, but I offer it just the same. It is easy to deflect criticism of oneself, particularly from the Bible, by quickly seeing it as applicable to others, and then concentrating on them and forgetting its accuracy in one's own case. Did the downgrading of the actual job of shepherding happen because the religious 'shepherds' could not take the passages as being critical of themselves? Did their knowledge of the Scripture not cause such passages to burn into the mind. And yet, 'God could not be criticising us ... we are doing a good job. It must be the real shepherds who are so to be despised.' Plausible?

Despised shepherds were: but it was to such rejected, devalued, objects of suspicion that the news of the birth of a Saviour was given. Take time out to read Luke 2:8-20 and note verse 11 in the light of what has just been said.

This is another example of what Jesus was talking about.
The angels brought the good news to a despised minority,
rejected by the powerful. Jesus himself sought out the man
who had been given back his sight, but had been rejected
by the Pharisees and told him of the Son of Man.

In his repeated use of the analogy, Jesus is therefore char-
acterising himself as an example of a good shepherd and,
by implication, the Pharisees as bad shepherds. In a way
we gain as much information by their inadequacies and
errors as we do from his affirmation about himself. The
negative renders the positive more striking by its contrast
with it. Further, the awful echoes of the Old Testament statements about the false shepherds and the glowing words
about the true shepherd add a perspective, giving depth to
Jesus' words. Uncaring and rejecting is juxtaposed with
care and love. Venal self-interest and self-absorption is
contrasted with the willingness of the true shepherd to lay
down his life for the sheep (John 10:15). Self-importance
is deflated by the presence of true importance. But we need
to look more closely at the elements.

In the first form of the story the thief and the robber
climb the wall to get into the sheep pen. The man who uses
the door is the true shepherd. The gate-keeper, presumably
recognising him, opens the door for him. The sheep hear
the shepherd's voice and follow him, but they will not follow someone whose voice they do not know. The true shepherd brings out his own, calling them by name, and going
before them (John 10:1-6).

From that version of the story it is clear that the true
shepherd is not a thief, that he has a flock which will follow him, and that he knows them. What has that to do with
the trigger of the story, the man born blind?

It is implicit in Jesus' words in John 9:3, when taken
along with the rest of the events of John 9, that the man

was one of Jesus' flock, one who, when called by name, followed his shepherd. The man had refused the other voices which had called to him, the Pharisees, which in Jesus' analysis implies that these were the voices of thieves. If that is so, are there other of the story's events which can be applied? How, for example, can one think of the ecclesiastics having climbed the wall of the sheep pen? It can only be that they had become or had made themselves religious leaders without in fact having been so commanded by God. We can take that right forward to today. How many men go through divinity school and into the ministry driven by their own will and without being truly called to that life? It is far preferable that a man's call to the ministry should come through the fellow-members of his congregation, with their becoming aware of the call to him through his work among the congregation, and perhaps even bringing the matter to his attention. The flock should have a part to play in verifying the call to any individual. In that way the genuinely spiritual call will be effective, but the spurious 'call' of what may in reality be a heavily disguised egotism, will be guarded against. How many ministers are in the wrong business? – a question which can work two ways.

The question then arises, in the first version of the story, who is the gate-keeper? I am not sure who opens the gate for the true shepherd, but I suspect it is God himself. It cannot be the 'prince of this world', for, if it were, the robbers would have no need to climb the wall. Certainly the Pharisees were not the gate-keepers. They did not recognise the true shepherd when he came: indeed, as Jesus said elsewhere, they shut up the kingdom of heaven, neither going in themselves, nor permitting others to enter (Matthew 23:13).

If I am not sure of the identity of the gate-keeper, I am sure why the gate is opened. It is opened to the true shepherd, allowing him access to his flock. In short, the claim of Jesus to be the good shepherd lies also within these words. As has been said, at the time there was a swelling current of praise of the good shepherds of the past, Moses and David being pre-eminent. Albeit elliptically, Jesus is claiming that title for himself. Perhaps at this point we could therefore refer straight through to the Messianic Shepherd figure in Zechariah and elsewhere, but let us first press on a little further.

The Door

It is in the second version of the story that Jesus uses the 'I AM' language. In the first version (John 10:1-6) he speaks impersonally. In the second he uses the direct 'I AM' formula: 'I am the gate'; 'I am the good shepherd.'

'I am the door' (I prefer the traditional words of the King James Version here) comes immediately in John 10:7 and again in verse 9. These two uses are, however, different. In verse 7 Jesus is the door which is a barrier between the sheep and the robbers. He is their *protection*. But, when in verse 7 he says that all who came before him were thieves and robbers, it is not clear whether he uses 'before' to mean earlier in time, or 'in front of'. However, this is not one of the times when we have to choose. Both possible meanings make sense, and can be accepted. There are times when scholars try to force an 'either/or' when the truth is 'both'. However, having said that, there is one point which may incline some to the spatial reference.

I have not seen in my reading a suggestion that the 'gate-keeper' of verse 3 and the gate of verse 7 can be run together, but they could. In Israel it was common for the shepherd, in the normal course of guarding his sheep in their pen by night, to sleep in the doorway. There were few physical doors, for timber was not plentiful. There were, therefore, few constructions of wood and nails to bar the access to the pen. Such were easily stolen and used for other purposes. Rather, it was the living body of the shepherd, and his light sleeping, which was the literal door of the sheep and their protection. And, if that is the case, it is also the reason why the thieves would climb the wall, not the gate.

Convincing? It has a definite appeal, and that is also why I suggested that the gate-keeper of the first version of the story was God. Jesus as the shepherd in the doorway is both gate-keeper and gate. Of course, on such a view, the question then arises, who is the man who proves to be the true shepherd? At that point I would simply retire with the plea that we are speaking of metaphors, not allegory: not every detail need fit so long as the message gets across. But if one persists with the notion of the sleeping shepherd as the gate, one can then by leaping logic associate the door with the door-posts and lintel splashed with the blood of the Passover Lamb which were the safety of the Israelites when the Angel of Death stalked through the land of Egypt (Exodus 12:1-7, 12-13, 22-23). There, in the mingled imagery of the door and the blood, the safety and the reason why there was safety for those inside, are other elements of the work of the true shepherd.

Protection is but one function of a door. Another is *access*. In this set of images Jesus is access into the safety of the sheep-fold. He is our access into God's fold. 'Whoever enters through me will be saved' (John 10:9). As we will see in Chapter 6, he is the Way, which includes the Way into the Holiest (Hebrews 9:8; 10:20).

That puts a contrast and a comparison into my mind. The contrast is with the gate of the Garden of Eden, shut and defended by cherubim and a flaming sword flashing back and forth (Genesis 4:24). No longer do we have access there. How far from such is Jesus, the door of the sheep. He welcomes those who would enter through him. The comparison is with the gates of the ancient cities of the Old Testament, which were the most important places in the town. They were the way in and out of the defences of the city. They were also where the elders sat in judgement and to discuss significant affairs. Lot's success in Sodom was shown by his becoming one who sat in its gate (Genesis 19:1). Boaz went there to gain Ruth by judicial settlement (Ruth 4:1-12). There are many other examples. Take any concordance and look through the references under 'gate' or 'door.' The gates of hell ... the gates of the Temple ... the gates of the city. Where to stop? One stops with Jesus, the gate of the sheep, for there is no other.

But Jesus speaks not only of access. He also speaks of the sheep going in and out to find pasture (John 10:9). As the Door he is the way out of the pen, governing the sheep's going out and in. We should only go out when he calls, he going before us as our shepherd, as verse 4 indicates. That implies some *training* or *discipline* for those sheep which will not heed his leading. Shepherds have ways of curbing straying sheep. One Israelite method was for the shepherd to break the foreleg of a persistent stray, and thereafter to care for it, carrying it around on his shoulder. The crippled sheep could no longer run away – indeed it could no longer run – and yet it was made the subject of a special tender care. The crippling was part of the fundamental process of caring for it through making sure that it learned the error of its ways. One can mull such images a long time. Sheep must learn to come and go only at the bidding of their shepherd, and, of course, the story makes it clear that they do recognise their master's voice.

A Possible Difference

One difference between the two versions of the story lies in the roles played by the sheep pen, the gate-keeper and the shepherd. In the second, as we have suggested, Jesus is the Door as well as the Good Shepherd, keeping his sheep safe within the pen. In the first version he comes to the gate which is opened for him, and calls his sheep out from among others. Is there anything to be gathered from this difference?

One view might be that there is a mixed flock in the first version, from which the shepherd calls out his own sheep by calling them by name. They recognise his voice, and follow. If this is the case then the sheep pen could have a variety of meanings. It could be the world at large, that generality of humanity from amongst which Jesus calls his own. In many of the other 'I AM' statements Jesus stresses that he has his own, given him by God, and whom he will not lose. Alternatively, but still with the underlying theme of selection from a larger group, the sheep pen might be the organised denominations of the world or any human society. Thus we have already suggested that it is likely that some of the Pharisees who were listening were called out from among the others even by this trenchant attack on their group (cf. John 10:21). Jesus says that he will call out his own from any pen in which he finds them: that they recognise his voice and follow is the mark that they are his. On such a view the gate-keeper, God, is keeping the pen (the world, church, group) in being and in safety for the protection of those sheep which are to be called out by the true shepherd. And such a view is scriptural.

A similar approach to the second version makes things even clearer. In that instance it is the shepherd who is in charge, Jesus being both shepherd and gate. The sheep go in and out of the pen, finding pasture at the command of the shepherd. The pen is, therefore, both their shelter and defence, and as such can only be a representation of Jesus' care for his own, though there is some attraction also in seeing this pen as the Church, the true assembly of all believers irrespective of denomination. That latter notion may seem to run into some difficulty with the notion of going in and out of it, but that is soluble by thinking of the pen as the believers gathered together – not as the mystic Church, but an assembly of the mystic Church.

It would seem therefore, that the two versions have a different, although considerably related, content. The first version is a picture of the liberation, collection and protection of Jesus' flock. He is talking of something like the mixed herd of Matthew 25:32, which is to be separated out at the Last Judgment. In the second version the emphasis lies on the protection of the whole flock belonging to the Good Shepherd, and on the protection and supervision of each sheep in its individual life as part of that herd.

But the two versions are not clearly severable from each other. In the first version there is the protection of the sheep-pen and the gate-keeper, which in many ways is not dissimilar from the protection by the shepherd in the second. Again, in the first version, when the shepherd calls out his sheep, we are not told in so many words whether there are any sheep left in the pen. That he brings out 'all his own' (John 10:4) does not explicitly indicate that there are some sheep which are not his own, and which are therefore left behind. On the other hand Jesus' reference to the Pharisees not heeding his voice because they are not his sheep, may argue that that is precisely what has happened. But then the Bible tends to contrast sheep and goats, not sheep and sheep. If one gives full play to that point, then the pen is emptied in version one, and the only points of difference between the variants relate to the person of the gate-keeper and his opening to the man who goes to the gate in version one, as contrasted with Jesus himself being both shepherd and gate in version two.

Therefore, it seems appropriate at this point to repeat something which is very important. We should not worry about trying to make the different metaphors and stories of the Bible into one self-consistent whole. It is the message which is consistent: the metaphors which occasionally carry it need not be. We need to harmonise the teaching, not the pictures, and learn when to drop the peripherals of the imagery. In the present case, it is true that Jesus calls his sheep to himself out of the world and that happens when they hear his voice and respond, becoming part of his flock. In another sense the separation from the world will only take place when he returns in glory. The Church is the company of believers. The world and the churches are kept in being by God for the good of the believers, allowing time for unborn generations to come to knowledge of him. These ideas do not necessarily conflict. But oppose them to each other, and try to attain a synthesis in which the accoutrements of the images are each given an equal prominence, and you hobble yourself, grossly inhibiting the degree to which you can appreciate the depth of any of the truths involved.

The Good Shepherd

Now, let us make the transition to the Good Shepherd himself. We have already noticed the source of such metaphors in the Old Testament. The Patriarchs, the founders of the race, Abraham, Isaac and Jacob were nomads, following their flocks. Lot had an eye to good grazing when given the choice of the Land by Abraham (Genesis 13:1-13, esp. 10-11). Job began with seven thousand sheep among his other wealth. The book ends with him having fourteen thousand sheep, and all his other riches similarly increased (Job 1:3; 42:12). In exile Moses was a shepherd (Exodus 3:1). David was a shepherd boy in the hills of Judaea (1 Samuel 16:11; 17:20; Psalm 78:70-72). God was the shepherd of his people, his flock (Psalms 79:13; 95:7; 100:3; Ezekiel 34:31; cf. Isaiah 40:11; Zechariah 10:3). The religious leaders of Jesus' day thought of themselves as the successors of Moses and David. Jesus ironically quotes a common saying encapsulating their attitude when he says, 'The teachers of the Law and the Pharisees sit in Moses' seat. So you must obey them' (Matthew 23:2). Yet these *soi-disant* leaders had depreciated the ancient calling of their exemplar, who spent one third of his life as a shepherd. To them, a shepherd was a churl.

The low status of actual shepherds in his day makes Jesus' use of the imagery of the Good Shepherd the more striking. He exalts the job. The shepherd cares for his flock. Going before it in the eastern manner, he seeks out pasture and water. He it is that finds the patches of grass and the springs of water in a bleak landscape and leads the flock to them (cf. Psalm 23 where the imagery is more poignant than the well-watered sheep lands of the West would allow). The Good Shepherd protects the flock from thief and wolf. If necessary, he gives his life for the sheep (John 10:11).

In evangelical circles, and where wolves are to be seen only in zoos, we have dimmed the brightness these images had when they were newly minted. Too soon we say: 'Ah, yes. Calvary. The shepherd laying down his life for the sheep.' It is not wrong to make that step, but that is not what Jesus was immediately saying to those who heard him speak of himself as the Good Shepherd. He is saying to those who had cast out the man born blind, that a good shepherd cares for his flock to the extent of dying for it. The hireling flees when danger threatens: he sees the wolf and runs. The Pharisees are challenged: which are they, shepherds or hirelings?

It is a question which many church members also ask when their minister, encountering some difficulty, seeks a new charge rather than staying and seeing things through. Paul solemnly warns the elders of the church at Ephesus that they are to be good shepherds of their flock, defending it against savage wolves, some of whom were to arise from within that very church itself (Acts 20:25-31). Peter also exhorts elders, shepherds of God's flock, to serve well, and does so in terms which echo the strictures of John 10 (2 Peter 5:1-4).

These are matters which concern sheep very much, but the under-shepherd is also himself a sheep, and is in as much need of salvation and care by the Good Shepherd as any of his flock. To all of us, therefore, Jesus' words regarding his sheep are welcome. It is a blessing to each of us that Jesus also reminds us that the good shepherd knows his sheep and that the sheep know his voice. To most of us one sheep looks much like another, but it is instructive to stand with a shepherd as his flock passes. He knows them with affection as individuals. I find it laugh-makingly appropriate that Jesus talks of himself in this way; that he is the Good Shepherd, but he does not call himself the good fisherman, though that picture would also be true. He called Andrew and Peter to be fishers of men (Matthew 4:19; Mark 1:17), but caught fish are such dead things. Shepherds can be friends with their sheep. Again and again the mutuality of knowledge is stressed. 'I know my sheep and my sheep know me' (John 10:14). The context carries us on to Calvary, but pause and savour the depths of these monosyllables. It is one of those short sentences which are like a limpid pool or a translucent gem – fire opal or moss agate, for choice.

Is it too great a thought for us? Are we too unworthy? The statement is made simply, as fact. The shepherd and the sheep know each other: I know my sheep and my sheep know me. We are not coyly or in spurious piety to turn down what Jesus says (cf. his reaction to Peter in Mark 8:32-33). His words are simple, direct, and give immense confidence. Of course, the knowing is not equal on both sides for we will never know him as he knows us, but there is a mutuality of knowing, which is an aspect of love. Certainty and security are in what he says in John 10:14-15 and again in verses 27-30. We are to listen to his voice, and follow. Yet at the same time there need be no fear of following an accomplished mimic who counterfeits Jesus' voice, for John 10:27-30 also makes it plain that the Father's hand as well as the Son's is involved.

Such thoughts also lead us to the parable of the Lost Sheep (Luke 15:1-7; cf. Ezekiel 34:12), where the focus on the shepherd does not obliterate the distress of the stray. If one is wondering whether one is hearing the right voice, or whether one is identifying the true shepherd among a babel of other alluring tones, then, yes, one should be like a lost sheep and bleat. Pray! But, when one has been found, one must stop bleating. The rescued sheep is restored to its position within the flock. And that is an important element in the story as well. We are not rescued or found so as to remain alone. Flocks are not masses of isolated individuals. The zoologists and agriculturalists have shown us that a flock is a socially organised group, with each member having a place and a role. To adapt Jesus' imagery, we see that within his flock we are each in some way shepherd to others, and are shepherded by others. We have each a place to fill, and duties of love to perform, and the way properly to be a sheep is to concentrate upon one's duties, not one's rights. Concentrate on one's rights and very soon Jesus' stinging rebuke to the Pharisees will likely be applicable to us as well.

Then, at the end of time, there will be one flock and one shepherd (John 10:16). But who and where are the 'other sheep' which are 'not of this fold', but which are also to be called? The most likely answer is that these are the Gentiles, though some have used the phrase to build theories of a galactic and indeed universal redemption (universal in the spatial not the theological sense). As to that, who can say? But I, and I dare say most of my readers, am not of the sheep-fold of Judah. We are of another flock, and have been called from that to the great flock. For us also has the Good Shepherd come. For us also he has laid down his life (John 10:17-18). For us also he has taken it up again (John 10:18). His rebuking of the Pharisees was justified: they had driven away the poor blind man, exactly one for whom they should have cared. Such a rebuke will never be justifiably directed at Jesus.

I am the gate; whoever enters through me will be saved (John 10:9).

I am the good shepherd; I know my sheep and my sheep know me (John 10:14).

My sheep listen to my voice; I know them and they follow me. I give them eternal life, and they shall never perish; no-one can snatch them out of my hand. My Father, who has given them to me, is greater than all; no one can snatch them out of my Father's hand. I and the Father are one (John 10:27-30).

CHAPTER 5

THE RESURRECTION AND THE LIFE

Now we enter a different world. From here on Jesus is talking to his own, to folk whom he knows. No longer is Jesus' audience the milling, questioning crowd to whom he spoke of the bread of life and the light of the world, nor is it the critical Pharisees for whom the diet had been the raw and bruising shepherd metaphors of the previous chapter. Nor is this audience the elementary class. It consists of people whom he had been teaching throughout the years of his public ministry. There is, therefore, less concession to mental or spiritual laziness, or to inability. While there will be some return to 'popular' imagery in the final picture, 'I am the true vine', we are first to go through 'the resurrection and the life,' and 'the way, the truth and the life'. Here then, as Jesus speaks to his intimates, truth is less refracted by the prism of his words. We are overhearing him with his advanced class.

Again, as before, we should note the context in which the words are spoken.

'I am the resurrection and the life' occurs in John 11:25. It is part of Jesus' response to what he has led Martha to say in verse 24. Their conversation is embedded in the story of the raising of Lazarus, and it would be handy were you now to read the full story of John 11:1-47, for the entire circumstances of this 'I AM' both antedate the death of Lazarus and continue after his being raised.

At the beginning of John 11, Lazarus, brother to Martha and Mary, lies sick in Bethany and the sisters send word of his illness to Jesus. There is no record of a request that Jesus should do something about the illness, but we can assume that this was in the sisters' minds. When later they meet Jesus, there is some indication they had expected some action in response to their message. Perhaps they hoped at least for his prayers. After all, when we tell a Christian that a close friend of his is ill, there is an expectation of prayer: why should the sisters' thought have been different? Nonetheless, the text does not indicate that Jesus was specifically asked to do anything, and certainly it is clear that he was not asked to come either to visit or to heal.

The disciples also do not seem to have expected Jesus to go to Bethany, and Martha and Mary probably shared their attitude. As John 11:8 shows, the disciples did not want their Master to go anywhere near those hostile Jews who were by now seeking his life. The last two confrontations with the Pharisees had been the last straw. Jesus had delivered that excoriating rebuke, couched in the imagery of the door and the good shepherd, and repeated it within the precincts of the Temple itself (John 10:25-30). We need to remember just how upset the Pharisees were by those analogies. For us 'the good shepherd' and 'the door' bear a pleasant and comforting message. For the Pharisees it was a stinging attack. And Jesus had added to it another claim to deity (John 10:30). The Pharisees were baffled and enraged, and the people had sought to stone him (John 10:31). Were he to turn up in Bethany, the Pharisees' posse would be out in force, and the disciples knew it. Bethany, less than two miles from Jerusalem (John 11:18), was too close to the headquarters of the Jewish authorities to be healthy (cf. John 11:16).

But in their reaction to the news that Jesus, after two days delay, was going to go to Bethany, the disciples were either rather forgetful, or had earlier suffered from a slight deafness, for, in response to the news of Lazarus's illness, Jesus had given a hint, albeit an ambiguous one. He said, 'This sickness will not end in death.' No, it is for God's glory so that God's Son may be glorified through it (John 11:4). That first sentence in the New International Version is more useful than the King James Version's 'This sickness is not unto death,' for it makes it clear that there was a prospective element involved. We are not to concentrate on whether Jesus' words meant that the illness would or would not be fatal. The point is that what was going to happen would be for the glory of God the Father and his Son. As we know, there would be death, but that would not be the end. Things would go through death to glory.

Is that a hint? It is, and it is one which the disciples should have caught. Indeed, maybe the disciples did have an inkling, for they did not try very hard to prevent Jesus from returning to Bethany. But it seems more likely that they just did not catch the inference of those words, although it was open to them to do so. They could have connected Jesus' words about the illness being for the glory of God with what Jesus had said about the man born blind (John 9:1-3). That whole episode with its marvellous revelation of the Good Shepherd had started with the disciples' question to their Master. Infected with the common notion that defects and illness have their root in sin personal or parental (tracing back to the Ten Commandments, Exodus 20:5), they asked whether the man had sinned, or whether his blindness was the result of his parents' sin. The answer was that the sin of neither the man nor his parents was the reason for the blindness. It had happened so that the work of God might be displayed (John 9:3). Jesus' reply to their question is therefore similar to his reaction to the news about Lazarus, though the wording is not as ex-

plicit as in that case. In Lazarus' case Jesus specifically
talks of glory to come out of the events: glory, not simply
the work of God.

The disciples were further to misunderstand. So, elliptically, and in words resonant of 'I am the light of the world',
Jesus tells them that he knows what he is doing (John 11:9-
10). He also tells them the true situation, although he still
uses indirect language. Lazarus is asleep and Jesus is going to wake him (verse 11). However, the disciples take his
words at face value. They share the common folk-lore trust
in the recuperative powers of sleep. If Lazarus is asleep, he
must be getting better (John 11:12); how true to our own
beliefs and to medical knowledge. Often sleep can be a
good sign, but sometimes it is not. This time it not only
was not a good sign, but things had gone beyond sleep, as
Jesus spells out for his friends. 'Lazarus is dead, and for
your sake I am glad that I was not there, so that you may
believe. But let us go to him' (John 11:14).

There is a question therefore – how did Jesus know that
Lazarus was dead? No matter: Jesus is going to deal with it.

This time the disciples do not object; perhaps the blunt
news of the death stunned them. At any rate all we have is
Thomas rather resignedly saying to the others, 'Come on
then. We too will go and die with our Master.' It is an odd
reaction, a sort of hopeless loyalty which is both deeply
touching and quite irrational. It is not a grand tragic ges-
ture, which might have had some nobility in it, but rather a
low-key resignation bordering on apathy.

And so, out of that sombre down-beat quietness we come
to some of the most marvellous minutes in the Bible, during which the budding faith of Martha flowers into an awe-
some statement of belief.

Hearing that Jesus has come, Martha leaves her sister in
the house in Bethany and goes out to meet him. Can you

picture John close by, listening? Or did he get Martha into a corner and grill her as to the ensuing conversation? Were there others who had gone out with her and overheard what was said between the two? It is intriguing to speculate, but we do not know, and it does not really matter. What matters is the actual conversation.

What is the intonation of the words Martha speaks? If you were acting the part of Martha, how would you phrase and inflect her side of the conversation? Had she heard of Jesus' response to their message? Had the sisters' messenger reported back to them Jesus' apparent unconcern at the news of Lazarus' illness? Is there a disappointed tone in her voice as she meets him?

Take the passage as a whole and you find that it would be unfair to have her start either sulky or carping. Nor is there disappointment here. Her words are serene, perhaps with a slight catch in the throat. She is stating fact. 'Lord, if you had been here, my brother would not have died. But I know that even now God will give you whatever you ask' (John 11:21-22). Contrast that with the later words of Mary. When, eventually, she comes out of the house she repeats Martha's first sentence and then stops (John 11:32). Is there not a difference between the two women?

Return to Martha's words. How extraordinary they are! Martha had some basis for the first sentence, for she knew of previous cases which Jesus had cured. She even had some basis for the second sentence, for she would have heard of the raising of the son of the widow of Nain (Luke 7:11-17), and the daughter of Jairus (Mark 5:21-43; Luke 8:40-56). But these would have been hearsay accounts. So far as we know she was not present on either of these occasions, and she does not mention them.

What would we have done in these circumstances? It would have been so tempting to criticise, like the later by-

standers at Lazarus's tomb: 'Could not he who opened the
eyes of the blind man have kept this man from dying?'
(John 11:37). The inference there is either that Jesus could
not have saved Lazarus, or worse, that he could have saved
him but chose not to do so. Indeed, the latter is true, though
not in the hateful meaning which the bystanders would have
given the words.

Or would we have sought to put other pressure on
Jesus? 'Look, can't you raise Lazarus for me like you did
the loved ones of Jairus and the widow? You were warned
he was ill, but you have come back too late to cure my
brother. In these circumstances, can't you bring him back
to life? You have done so for others who have less claims
of friendship on you.'

Does that sort of plea ring a bell? Or am I wrong? Was
Martha just being indirect, like so many, not saying what
she actually meant? Was she being shifty, cunning,
manipulative, manoeuvring, without the guts, courage or
honesty to be plain? Is this not that horrid perversion,
'diplomacy', which is light years removed from true
diplomacy? Is this an attempt to corner Jesus and use him?
A way to arm-lock him into doing what was unsaid, but
deeply desired?

I cannot find anything in Martha's words or behaviour
which can fairly be described by any such epithets. The
explanation of her words is simple. There was in her a bud
of faith, as yet unopened, but trembling on the verge of its
spring. Jesus knows it, and draws it out.

'Your brother will rise again.'

'I know that he will rise again at the resurrection at the
last day' (John 11:23-24).

There was a foundation for these words of Martha, hesi-
tant though they might be. The orthodox pharisaic teaching of the time was that there would be a resurrection of

the dead at the last day. Although there is very little on the resurrection in the Old Testament, the Pharisees had by then discovered it and brought it out.

But that hope was not Martha's real hope. Her words contain a give-away as to her true feelings. Hesitantly she has responded to Jesus. I retract nothing about her not being devious or accusatory. She is shyly hoping against hope, and wondering at his words. She *knows* Jesus. She knew his miracles, the cures, and even the bringing back of the dead to life. She trusts Jesus, and as the Psalmist says, she is casting her burden on him (cf. Psalm 55:22). She knew of his care for her, and she was leaving this burden with him. Yet, even so, she did prefer one outcome rather than the other.

Consider Jesus' words: 'Your brother will rise again.' That is an unqualified statement, but without any indication of when Lazarus might rise from the dead. As in the case of so many of Jesus' statements, it was simply accurate. How were *those* words spoken? What was their tone, pace, and inflection? Try to act out that exchange:

'Your brother will rise again.'

'I know that he will rise again in the resurrection at the last day.'

Are her words tentative? 'Lord I know about *that*; and that *could* be what you are meaning. But do you mean something more?'

And then, as the glory of the rising sun, and as sudden as a master composer modulates into a magnificent melody, Jesus replies: 'I am the resurrection and the life. He who believes in me will live, even though he dies; and whoever lives and believes in me will never die. Do you believe this?' (John 11:25-26).

Martha's response is immediate, and soaring: 'Yes, Lord,' she told him. 'I believe that you are the Christ [the Mes-

siah], the Son of God, who was to come into the world'
(John 11:27).

Martha had penetrated the message of the Old Testament. She encapsulates and summarises the whole matter
in those few words. Jesus is the Messiah. She does not say:
'I believe you are the resurrection and the life, whatever
you mean by that odd expression.' No. It is straight through
to the heart of the matter: the Christ who was to come has
come.

Then see what she does; here again is practical Martha.
She does not hang about, wallowing in her flight of faith.
She goes to get her sister, and does so in such a kind way:
'The Teacher is here and is asking for you' (John 11:28).
She has got her priorities right. She does not keep Jesus to
herself, but gets her beloved sister to share. So often we
contrast Martha and Mary, Martha the busy one, irritated
with her sister who has been sitting listening to Jesus; Mary
has chosen the better part (Luke 10:38-42). This time it is
Martha who has got it right.

The sisters' reaction to Jesus does make a contrast. I get
the feeling from verse 20 that Mary deliberately did not go
out to meet Jesus with Martha, but waited to be asked. If I
were called on to deliver her words of verse 32 I would
make them somewhat sullen, even resentful, her mourning
the death of her brother notwithstanding. Yes, Mary does
fall at Jesus' feet (verse 32), and Martha did not. Yes, Mary's
weeping was to touch Jesus deeply (verse 33). Yes, Martha
lapses into her practical manner very soon. When Jesus
orders the gravestone to be removed from the grave-mouth
Martha warns and perhaps even objects. The New International Version is too polite. 'There will be a stink.' But all
that is as nothing compared with her words of faith, and
Mary's relative silence. Let us give Martha her due.

Jesus' words to Martha are intriguing. He does not say,

'If you live and believe in me you will not die.' He says, 'He who lives and believes in me will not die.' There is a difference, and it is an important one. The first formulation is a contractual statement; the second a statement of fact. Jesus is not saying, 'If you do this, you will be entitled to have that happen. All will be well if only you work yourself up into a lather of belief.' Now I know that there are other passages and verses such as Paul and Silas saying to the Philippian jailer, 'Believe in the Lord Jesus Christ and you shall be saved, you and your household' (Acts 16:31). But I am not convinced that Paul's words are conditional, in the legal sense – if you do this you will have right to that. Such words as Paul's can also be construed as simple statements of fact. The two matters, belief and salvation, go together. They are a package, and are not causally linked. You cannot have one without the other, but the other is not linked to the one by an obligation laid on God through or by the one. We have already seen this in other of Jesus' words. Again and again in the 'light of the world' and in the 'good shepherd' passages he says that he knows those who are his, and that they are given him by the Father. He will lose none of them (cf. the High Priestly prayer in John 17). We are to take such words with care, but keep them together as a unit, as a whole. Analytically to separate and then to intrude a false causal link pulls the idea apart and kills it. You cannot post-mortem something living. Belief and eternal life go together.

I believe that Martha takes Jesus' words in that simple way, holding the two elements together in a confident trust, and we should follow her example. His affirmation 'I am the resurrection and the life' unfolds that bud of faith in her heart and she realises that for her he is the Christ. She does not 'believe' and he 'becomes'. She realises that for her he *is*. He is the resurrection and the life. And with that

deep security she can turn to other things. She can go off
and fetch her sister. For herself, and all that she cares about,
all is well. All is well even if Lazarus moulders in his grave.
Indeed, having typed that last sentence, I wonder whether
it was entirely fair even faintly to suggest that Martha's
objection to the opening of the grave was a lapse of some
sort. Might it not be that in her new realisation of her Saviour, Martha had accepted her brother's death, and the physiological consequences of four days in a hot country?

At the grave Jesus kindly turns aside her objection. Yes,
he wept on approaching the tomb (John 11:35), but is there
not now a hint of humour in his words to Martha? 'Did I
not tell you that if you believed you would see the glory of
God?' (John 11:40). Well, no. Not in the text we have. So it
is plain that John omits some of the conversation with
Martha. Or were the words of verse 40 said to the disciples, recalling to them his words on receiving the news
that Lazarus was ill? I do not know. Whatever the answer
to these questions, the glory of God was about to be shown
to those present, and that not ineffectively. Following the
raising of Lazarus, many were to believe, and that was further to madden the chief priests (John 11:45; 12:9-11).

On Jesus' instructions the stone is rolled away, either by
the disciples or by some of the bystanders. Jesus prays to
his Father, and then calls on his friend to come forth. Lazarus does (John 11:41-44). (One wonders how the bystanders reacted.) 'Take off the grave clothes and let him go.'
The man is freed, and, we assume, goes back to live as
normal a life as he can after such an experience and such a
public restoration.

Leading a completely normal life would have been difficult, of course, and probably impossible. In the next chapter we learn that Lazarus was an object of curiosity for
some time (John 12:9). It also tells us something horrific.

As we saw in the last chapter, the man born blind and cured by Jesus was driven out by the Pharisees, but that was from their examination of him, and it seems he was not excluded from society or the village where he lived. They did not care for him, but their reaction was what we might call passively negative. Now, because many were believing in Jesus after the raising of Lazarus, the chief priests decided that Lazarus as well as Jesus should be done away with (John 12:9-11). How depraved! How ungenerous! How unfeeling! How unhuman! To plot to kill a man because he has been raised from the dead! Given history, it is unfortunately conceivable that such an atrocity should have been contemplated. Its only explanation, though not its excuse, is the by then devil-inspired opposition to Jesus.

So much for the story. We now need to think further about the content of the words, 'I am the resurrection and the life.' We have gone round them, and taken their content for granted, but when we turn properly to face them, their meaning is so glorious that it is difficult to concentrate on. Just as one cannot see the sun, nor perceive detail when looking into the light, so it is difficult to think, let alone write of such matters. It is tempting to escape into academic reflection and thereby to insulate oneself from their power and impact.

What was the nature of Lazarus's being brought back to life? He certainly was not resurrected, but rather he was resuscitated, for, unlike Jesus, he was later to die again. Or did he die at all the first time? Is the fact that he had not decayed these four days in the heat not evidence that he was in a coma? Or had he decayed, but was somehow restored by Jesus' command? Such questions are a barrier, an excuse and an escape. Jesus said that Lazarus was dead, making it clear that he was not asleep, when the disciples misunderstood his more gentle initial phraseology. We are

not told that Lazarus was resurrected, only that he was dead
and was raised. Jesus' resurrection was to be different.
Lazarus raised was not Lazarus resurrected. There is no
causal link between Jesus' words to Martha and the raising. Let us not be evasively academic, but take these things
as they are given.

When Jesus spoke to Martha (perhaps with the disciples crowding round, for they would have arrived together),
what was he saying to her? As with the other 'I AM' statements, some content can be gleaned by using knowledge
from the Old Testament. In this case, however, there is not
very much that would have sprung to mind. Instead of the
manifold associations of such words as 'I am the light of
the world', there are only a few passages which would have
seemed relevant. But we are privileged, and look on such
matters from a different stand-point in time. We have much
more to inform our thinking, but for the present let us see
what might have then been seen.

Old Testament Revelation

For the Jew of Jesus' time the only unequivocal reference
to resurrection comes in Daniel 12:2 where the prophet
sees that: 'Multitudes who sleep in the dust of the earth
will awake: some to everlasting life, others to shame and
everlasting contempt.' The context of that resurrection is
the time of distress and the judging of the people, and clearly
Martha referred to that occasion in her first reply to Jesus'
enigmatic prompting.

Of course there are also less obvious hints of resurrection in the Old Testament. There is Job's great affirmation:
'I know that my Redeemer lives, and that in the end he will
stand upon the earth. And after my skin has been destroyed,
yet in my flesh I will see God; I myself will see him with

my own eyes – I and not another' (Job 19:25). There is Ezekiel's vision of the valley of dry bones (Ezekiel 37). Hosea also knows something, though his vision is patchy (Hosea 6:1-3; 13:14). So does Isaiah (Isaiah 26:19; 38:17), and various Psalms hint at a confidence which sometimes passes beyond an earthly salvation (e.g. Psalms 16; 30:2-3, 9-12; 49:15; 73:24; 86:12-13; 88:5, 10-12; 103: 1-4; 116:8).

Such passages, therefore, provided a base on which the Pharisaic belief in resurrection developed. Naturally it was a doctrine which was welcomed, and spread quickly among the people, being sufficiently well-established in the popular mind to allow the Sadducees to question Jesus about the wife of the seven brothers (Luke 20:27-40) – a mischievous question, for the Sadducees did not themselves believe in the resurrection.

Yet Jesus' words to Martha are so different from the Pharisaic notion. And indeed the distinction we made earlier between a contractual view of the relationship between God and man, and the true relationship with Christ, had strange echoes in orthodox opinion at the time Jesus spoke. Jesus' words depart from the Pharisaic thinking on the matter. The Pharisees certainly based their thoughts upon the passages we have mentioned, but they had also bolstered it with an intellectual reasoning. Their confidence was rooted in the premise that by obeying the commands of God one obtained 'eternal life.' The question to Jesus, 'What shall I do to inherit eternal life?' (Mark 10:17), with its implication of eternal life deserved as a reward for good conduct, was natural to their way of thinking. They saw a good life as having to do with fulfilling one side of a bargain. If one lived right, according to the Law, then God would protect and bless. He had promised. But it went further than that. The Pharisees considered that if one did

obey God, God's fulfilment of the extravagant promises of
blessing he had made as being his side of the bargain just
could not be crammed into the span of an earthly life. It
would take an eternal lifetime for that to happen. Hence,
what Daniel and the others indicated were what they seemed
to be: intimations of a resurrection, a resurrection to everlasting life for the obedient. The prophecies and revela-
tions were 'proved' by such intellectual deductions.

We have already explored Jesus' contrasting formulation of the matter (John 11:25-26). What the Pharisees saw
as their entitlement for their obedient performance of the
terms of a contract, Jesus presents as the necessary result
of a true relationship with himself.

The simplicity of Jesus' words is striking of itself. He
relates belief and eternal life without further complication.
We should also, however, seek to appreciate his words in
their context, as directly relating to Martha and those who
may have overheard them, and also more generally as relating to ourselves.

To appreciate the impact of what Jesus said on his immediate hearers we need to remember what things were
like in those days. Lazarus had died, but that was not something that could not have happened. Recall the way in which
the disciples had taken the news of his illness and then
death. Life expectancy was short. Death was frequent and
swift. Everyone knew about it and encountered it often.
There were no antiseptic and clinical hospitals where, as
today, the individual could pass from the sight of his friends
and relations to be delivered briefly back to them, pretti-
fied by the undertaker's craft in a formal, elegant casket.
Death happened in the home, often as the result of a ravag-
ing disease. Funeral processions were a common sight in
the streets, often without coffins. Death was frightening
and unpleasant. A certainty of resurrection was therefore

something to strike home to all, conscious as each was of the uncertainty of his own life.

Yet it may be that I make too much of those circumstances as speaking particularly to the people of Jesus' day. Death is today dreaded by many, even though dying takes place mostly in private, and the burial ceremonies are stylized, sanitised and anaesthetising. Death's very unfamiliarity makes it terrifying. To cease to be is not something we readily contemplate. We try to forget about it, and yet it keeps coming back particularly as what we elliptically and symptomatically call 'intimations of mortality' come upon us. In such circumstances it is good to know of eternal life, but that then brings with it the fear of what that life will be. The knowledge of judgment is deep-rooted in the human psyche despite the efforts of our modern atheist soothsayers. It is therefore marvellous to hear what Jesus said is the basis of resurrection to life, to know that it depends on belief in him as the resurrection and the life (John 11:25-26). It does *not* depend upon our fulfilling our side of a bargain. That is a great relief, with at least two consequences.

First, it would not be comfortable to think that one's eternal welfare is based on the always doubtful result of a balance-sheet of one's obedience and right living set against sin, conscious and unconscious. One cannot rely on the assurance given by some prelate or other. By contrast the certainty of eternal life based upon faith in a person whom one knows frees the spirit. See again Martha's soaring words: how *were* they delivered?

Second, if that resurrection promise is trustworthy, we need to remember it brings with it all those references in the Old Testament to eternal life, transforming them as a jewel suddenly flames when caught in a shaft of light. Resurrection and life go together as Jesus says. 'He who believes in me will live, even though he dies; and whoever lives and believes in me will never die' (John 11:25). Living in Jesus, living after death, believing in him; these are all intertwined.

Eternal life, though death may intervene: that is the promise of Jesus to Martha and through her to all of us, for his words are general. That death may intervene is shown by the later death of Lazarus. Unless Christ comes first, we will all go into the grave before being called forth in our turn. But, while there is life in Christ after death, there is also life in Christ before death, and that is a blessing not to be dissipated. We are not putting in time waiting for the crematorium van to come along.

Believers live in Christ now, from day to day and moment to moment, whether or not we are conscious of it. We are not to sink into passive contemplation, but are to remember whose we are. Martha spoke her confession, and went and did something for someone else. She went back into her pattern of life – it was transformed, and there were glitches and hiccups to come – but it was her pattern of life.

So, in ending this chapter, let a question be asked. Since Jesus has said to me, and to you, 'Lazarus, come forth into life,' why do we neglect the other thing he also said? (Yes, it was said to bystanders, but surely the man himself helped.) 'Take off the grave clothes and let him go.' We are not to be trammelled with the grave clothes of old sinful habits and preoccupations. We are to put on wedding garments, not stay in the cerements of our fallen nature, the Old Adam. We are to be free in him.

So, now, can you deliver these words properly? Those who can must live their truth:

'Lord, if you had been here my brother would not have

died. But I know that even now God will give you whatever you ask.'

'Your brother will rise again.'

'I know he will rise again in the resurrection at the last day.'

'I am the resurrection and the life. He who believes in me will live, even though he dies; and whoever lives and believes in me will never die. Do you believe this?'

'Yes, Lord. I believe that you are the Christ, the Son of God, who was to come into the world' (John 11: 21-27).

CHAPTER 6

THE WAY, THE TRUTH AND THE LIFE

Once again we need to start with context.

'And it was night.' Like the slamming of a dungeon door at the far end of a long corridor, the second sentence of John 13:30 echoes down the centuries. Judas has gone out to betray his Master, 'And it was night.' Nonetheless and extraordinarily, the mood within the Upper Room immediately lifts. There is relief in Jesus' words:

> Now is the Son of Man glorified and God is glorified in him. If God is glorified in him, God will glorify the Son in himself, and will glorify him at once. My children, I will be with you only a little longer. You will look for me, and just as I told the Jews, so I tell you now: Where I am going, you cannot come (John 13:31-33).

The first sentences are buoyant. The last moment at which Judas might have turned back has been reached, and passed. The train of events has gone past the last points. Calvary is inevitable. Jesus knows it, and the strain of uncertainty has gone.

It is in that context of relief, amounting to relaxation, that 'the way, the truth and the life' is drawn from Jesus as part of the discussion of the disciples impending inability to follow where he was going. The statement does not, however, emerge immediately. First Jesus speaks of the new commandment, 'Love one another' (John 13:34-35). How-

ever, Peter takes up the previous point about their not being able to follow but then, before that can be explored,
stumbles into the prophecy of his betrayal of his Master
(John 13:36-38). Not until the next chapter does the question of where Jesus is going recur, and that is where it gives
rise to the 'I AM' statement.

In passing, note a further contribution to our apprecia-
tion of the circumstances in which Jesus made the various
'I AM' proclamations. Once more in the course of the conversation the disciples show their crass ability to avoid the
important and go for the irrelevant, their capacity to stall
at a preliminary point. Think of it. It is true that Jesus has
spoken of his going from them, and that would have been a
matter of great concern, but surely his command about love
deserved more attention? Surely they should have been
taken up with that? Jesus states it so fully:

> 'A new command I give you: Love one another. As I have
> loved you, so you must love one another. All men will
> know that you are my disciples if you love one another'
> (John 13:34-35).

But the instruction was to strike home only later. Jesus'
words were to bear blessed fruit in the epistles of John,
suffused as they are with the duty and privilege of love. If
John the Elder (2 John 1; 3 John 1) was not John the Apostle, then John the Apostle must have fairly hammered the
message into him. So Jesus' instruction to love one another did stick, but not immediately. Instead the disciples
lock onto the other (arguably the lesser) question: 'Where
are you going, Lord?'

Does that not speak volumes? Be clinical about it. Most
Christian messages and sermons exhort, 'Love one another,'
and yet so swiftly the mind attaches itself to something
else. Anything is more comfortable than the simple instruc-

tion to 'love one another'. Is it that we dimly realise how far that instruction goes beyond the superficial, and therefore seek refuge in other, more comfortable matters? Or do we even recognise what we do? Do we think that such an instruction is obeyed by our being sweet to one another? Is 'love' for us an emotional surge, and one which can be conjured up to order? It must be none of these, for Jesus is speaking of the true love of God flowing through us to our fellows. We must not hinder him. And indeed Jesus does return to such matters later in John 14:15-21, so the point is not lost sight of, but in the interim he allows the disciples their head. Where *is* he going?

The words which trigger their inquiry are intriguing in themselves. Jesus says that he will not be with them much longer, that they will look for him, and that they cannot go where he is going (John 13:33). He adds that he has told the Jews similar things before. What then had he said to the Jews?

Two occasions on which Jesus used similar enigmatic words to the Jews are John 7:33-34 and John 8:21. In the first Jesus had been teaching in the Temple at the time of the Feast of Tabernacles. The chief priests and the Pharisees, disturbed by reports of his teaching, sent the temple guards to arrest him. In retrospect, given our knowledge of the Gospels, his response is clear to us, but see his exact words:

'I am with you for only a short time, and then I go to the one who sent me. You will look for me, but you will not find me; and where I am, you cannot come' (John 7:33-34).

The words are almost exactly what he was later to say to the disciples, and they certainly took the attention of his immediate audience when they were said. 'Where does this man intend to go that we cannot find him? Will he go where our people live, scattered among the Greeks, and teach the Greeks? What did he mean by, "You will look for me, but you will not find me," and "Where I am, you cannot come"?' (John 7:35-36)

Fascinating, isn't it! Will he go to the Greeks? – Yes, and beyond, to the Gentiles, to the north-east corner of Scotland, across the prairie, through mountain regions and jungle, to the islands and the farthest continents.

But that was for the far future. Even in the life of most of his hearers, however, there was to be a fulfilment of his words. It is another example of his strict, if elliptical, accuracy. After his resurrection, were they not to look for him and find no trace of him? There is no record of an actual search party sent out by the authorities, but the tomb was reported empty, and the authorities did suborn the guards to report that the body had been stolen (Matthew 28:11-15). Was there no attempt to find the corpse, the production of which would have shattered the spreading story of his rising from the grave? Perhaps the authorities knew they would not find one ...?

However, what we are seeking is what the disciples should have remembered as instances of when Jesus had previously spoken of these things to the Jews. One of these is in the passage which we have just quoted. Jesus told the Jews in John 7:33 that he was to 'go to the one who sent' him. That is only a short phrase among the many discussions with the Jews which the disciples would have listened to, so are we being unfair in pointing it out? Perhaps, and perhaps not. Would the disciples have assumed that they would always accompany their Master when he was speaking in such clear terms to the Jews of going away? Given what else we have learned of the disciples, it may be that it never crossed their minds that they also were to be left behind, but if we accept that possibility, it does leave them as rather unreflective souls.

The other record of Jesus talking of his departure to the Jews comes in John 8, just after one of the 'light of the world' statements. At John 8:13 the Pharisees challenge Jesus on the ground that he is testifying to himself and the ensuing discussion contains many strains. Out of it we can pick the matter of Jesus' going somewhere else. Thus at verse 14 he says, '... I know where I came from and where I am going. But you have no idea of where I come from or where I am going.' Then, perhaps on the same occasion, or at least shortly thereafter, he says, 'I am going away, and you will look for me, and you will die in your sin. Where I go, you cannot come' (John 8:21). The Jews therefore began to question among themselves, 'Will he kill himself? Is that why he says "Where I go you cannot come"?' (John 8:22). They are, therefore, that much nearer to the truth: he will die – but at their hand. And Jesus responds, mystifying them further: 'You are from below; I am from above. You are of this world; I am not of this world. I told you that you would die in your sins; if you do not believe that I am the one I claim to be, you will indeed die in your sins' (John 8:23-24).

'Who are you?' they demand in reply. How should we inflect that cry? Does it contain anguish, exasperation or contempt? Jesus replies once more that he is who he has been saying he is. His Father is reliable, and he has said nothing which he has not heard from the Father. When they have killed him they will then know that he does nothing of himself, but only what the Father pleases (John 8:25-29). (It is good to note in passing that as a result of this confrontation many put their faith in him, John 8:30.)

These passages, then, are reported instances where Jesus had spoken of his going somewhere where he could not be followed. It may be unfair to suggest that the disciples could have remembered them in the highly charged atmosphere of the Upper Room, but it does seem that Jesus gently rebukes their questioning of him. He had spoken of these things before (John 13:33). Or was it that, as had been said, they perhaps had not appreciated that they too were excluded from following him?

Irrespective of these speculations, it remains true that from these indications given earlier to the Jews we can glean certain things. There was a place to which Jesus was going. It was above. He had come from there, and was going back to it. He was here only a short time, and was to return to him who had sent him. Even if you strip away John's comments, made as he later wrote the story down in his Gospel, these elements are all plain in Jesus' reported words. Occasionally John does underline the point for us, for example that Jesus was talking of the Father (John 8:27), but even if you ignore his prompting, the material is not thereby diminished.

That being so, why did Peter have to ask where Jesus was going (John 13:36)? And what is the explanation of Thomas's almost petulant outburst: 'Lord, we don't know where you are going, so how can we know the way?' (John 14:4). It quite shatters the mood engendered by the initial verses of chapter 14, hallowed at so many Christian gravesides, 'Let not your heart be troubled ...' with its promise of 'many mansions'. Thomas's question, or complaint, seems quite out of place coming as it does immediately after Jesus has said that he goes to prepare a place for them, and that they know the way (John 14:3-4). Indeed, really Thomas directly contradicts what Jesus has just said.

If I look deep within myself, I can see an answer to those questions. The disciples had been three years with Jesus, listening to his teaching as he instructed them, and as he spoke more generally to the Jews. Such as John were drinking in the teaching and the whole events of his ministry to such effect that years later they were able to write their Gospels. Others were able to fill Luke's notebooks as he went round interviewing everyone he could before starting his account for Theophilus (Luke 1:1-4). Yet, despite their interest, at crucial points and times of stress some things simply dropped out of their reckoning. They forgot, just when it would have been useful to have remembered. How like us! What use have we made of the opportunity to learn, not merely head-knowledge, but heart-knowledge, making the good news part of oneself so that it does not lift like the morning dew in the heat of a crisis? What was written earlier about the importance of regular harvesting of manna (see Chapter 2) comes to mind.

Yet Jesus is so forgiving. His reply to Thomas is not the terse, 'I am the way, the truth and the life,' which it could have been. That would have been a put-down, a conversation stopper and a rebuke all rolled into one. Instead his reply is gentleness itself, though it is not the easier for all that, and his reply rolls on through Philip's intervention, and on down to the end of John 14. Its kernel, however, lies for our purposes in verses 6-7. Jesus answered [Thomas], 'I am the way, the truth and the life. No one comes to the Father except through me. If you really knew me, you would know my Father as well. From now on, you do know him and have seen him' (John 14:6-7). (There is also an intriguing variation for the third sentence given in the British edition of the New International Version: 'If you really have known me, you will know the Father as well,' a translation which triggers its own thoughts.)

The kernel is knowing God. We are not, like some modern theologians, saying farewell to a formerly helpful concept which we have now outgrown. We are getting to know God through Christ, through Christ in our hearts, in our

Bibles and in other Christians. That is the import of Jesus'
correction of Philip in the succeeding verses, and in the
broadening out of the teaching in the rest of the chapter,
even to encompass the promise of the Holy Spirit at verses
16-17. But it is all in verses 6-7. Jesus is in the Father and
the Father is in him. To know him is to know the Father. We
are, therefore, in the midst of profound and almost confus-
ing ideas: the Incarnation, the indwelling Christ, God the
Father, Son and Holy Spirit, God the Creator and Sustainer,
the Redeemer ... all these bound up in the person of the
man Jesus. Reason turns to contemplation.

So let us step back a little. Contemplation can turn into
a trance, and it is precisely to prevent our sinking into a
morass that Jesus gave those word pictures of himself. Their
purpose was to transpose certain truths about him down
into a more easily graspable form. Only by putting some
content into the phrases can we hope to escape the easy,
comfortable wallow which is the preliminary to spiritual
torpor. The 'I AM' statements are tools. Jesus is the way,
the truth and the life. What do the bits mean?

The Way

'The way' is a curious expression. Of course it has roots,
as we shall see, but it is not a transparent expression, in-
stantly carrying obvious meaning in this context. On the
contrary it is rather opaque. Nonetheless, 'the way' was
the main expression which was shortly to identify the nas-
cent church. Paul, when he was as yet only Saul, pressed
on up the road to Damascus, bearing his letters of commis-
sion from the High Priest himself, authorising him to root
out any whom he might find there who were 'of the Way',
or of 'that Way' (Acts 9:2). When later that same Paul,
now of the Way himself, was at Ephesus 'there arose a great

disturbance about the Way', with Demetrius stirring up the silversmiths (Acts 19:23). Finally, Paul himself, on trial before the governor Felix, admits that he is 'a follower of the Way, which they [the Jews] call a sect' (Acts 24:14). 'The Way' was therefore followed by the early Christians before they came to be called Christians at all, that latter term being first applied to them in Antioch (Acts 11:26). Paul's confession to Felix proves that the previous label continued in common use for some time thereafter, and it is still claimed by one or two modern sects as their own appellation.

The notion of a 'way' is not unusual in general religious parlance. There are upward and downward ways, higher ways and lower ways, left-hand and right-hand paths, and so on. We are easy with the phrase a 'way of life'. We are familiar with a 'cross-roads'. In all these phrases we draw on a common store of religious language, but there may be more to it than that. I am intrigued by the notion (which I first cogently encountered in C. S. Lewis' *The Pilgrim's Regress*) that other religions do contain echoes and glimpses of the truths of Christianity. Could the generality of the notion of 'a way' be explicable on the ground that there actually is 'the way'?

Of course, within the Old Testament there are many uses and analogues of the idea. Exodus is the Way Out (*ex-hodos*), the way out from the slavery of Egypt to the Promised Land. The Redeemer, the Holy One of Israel, is therefore 'he who made a way through the sea, a path through the mighty waters' (Isaiah 43:14,16). Throughout the Psalms we read of the way laid out for man by God (e.g. Psalms 1:6; 5:8-9; 18:21, 30, 32; 25:5, 8-10; 31:3; 37:5; 86:11; 103:7; 139:24). The very first verses of Psalm 119 state a recurring theme of that paean of praise, 'walking in the ways of the LORD.' Isaiah cries in words which fore-

shadow those of John the Baptist: 'The voice of one calling: "In the desert prepare the way for the LORD, make
straight in the wilderness a highway for our God" ' (Isaiah
40:3), and it is notable that all four Gospels report John the
Baptist's proclamation of these terms (Matthew 2:3; Mark
1:3; Luke 3:4-6; John 1:23). Is this another example of the
disciples seeing connections later, of their being wise after
the event and remembering Jesus, the Way? Whatever the
explanation, each writer places early in his account that
cry of the ancient prophet being duly taken up on cue by
the herald of the Lord.

There are other phrases as well, phrases to which we
have been accustomed, even inured. There is the way of
holiness, the way of the Lord, the way in which God leads
the willing, and so on. But Jesus' phrase is different. It
takes all these familiar expressions and shows that they are
not quite right. Jesus, the person, is the way in a manner
that his teaching is not. The Way of the early church was
not a following of traditions handed on through the recita-
tion of the teaching of a rabbi. Nor was it the repetition of
the doctrines in which others had expressed their understanding of the teachings and of the man himself. The Way
was following Jesus himself. We are asked to follow Jesus,
not a system of doctrine. Dear Philip, 'Believe me when I
say that I am in the Father and that the Father is in me; or at
least believe on the evidence of the miracles' (John 14:11).
Begin with the miracles if you must, but come on through
them to know the Father and the one for who they are. Begin with the teaching if you must, some formal system of
doctrine expressing an understanding of holy things, but
see through it all to the living God who stands behind it.

And, implicit in that and in John 14 itself, there is the
corollary. To follow the teaching, to be word-perfect in the
doctrine, to score one hundred and one per cent in theol-

ogy exams and yet not to make contact with the God-Man himself is, in the last resort, to reject the teaching, the doctrine and the knowledge. To divide between Jesus and his teaching, and to refuse to bridge between his words and himself, requires that one selects what one will follow, leaving oneself as judge in these matters. You are then your own god, or demon. Recall Bunyan's *Pilgrim's Progress*.

Some considerable way on their journey, Christian and Hopeful meet Ignorance, who has just come down a crooked lane from the country of Conceit and got into the Way (!) without entering it by the wicket-gate which marks its beginning. Ignorance thinks that all will be well with him, for he fasts and pays his tithes. His view is, however, that each should be content to follow the religion of his own country, for do not the ways from all countries lead to the same end point as that from Christian's country? Well, they do, and it does. But, on the very last page of my copy of the *Progress*, on the orders of the King, Ignorance is seized by angels from the City and is thrown down a chute to hell from just outside the gate of heaven. Why? Because Ignorance does not know the Lord, and carries no certificate of citizenship of the heavenly kingdom. He did not know Jesus, though he had apparently followed his way right to the gate. He had never met Jesus (cf. Matthew 7:22-23).

Jesus, then, is the Way; not what he said or what his disciples later wrote about him, nor what is on the miles of theology shelves (including this book too). He himself is the Way. But, that warning given, there are other elements in the idea of the way which we can bring out.

Mention has already been made of the Exodus as the way out of Egypt, and of the occasions on which the teaching and leading of God are said to be his way. God's words are a path to the feet and light to the eyes (cf. Psalm 119:101, 104, 105), but that way is not an aimless, wandering way.

A way is a road going somewhere. There is an acute sense of purpose in the notion. A road itself goes nowhere, but it becomes a way when an individual gets onto (into?) it and uses it to go somewhere. When we set foot in a street, an avenue or a boulevard, that is the way to our destination. It is the same with Christ, the Way.

Jesus, the Way, is going to his Father. As he said to the Jews, he is going to him who sent him (John 7:33), and he reminds the disciples of that fact. He is going to his Father's house to prepare a place for his disciples (John 14:3). He is going to the Father, and yet he is in the Father and the Father is in him even as he speaks to them. There is a curious penetration and urgency in Philip's cry, 'Show us the Father and that will be enough for us' (John 14:8). There is also a blindness. The Father is present in the Son already (John 14:10-11), and they had heard him say to the Jews 'I and my Father are one' (John 10:30). It cannot be that that statement had made no impression, even though it comes tagged on at the end of the second major use of the imagery of the good shepherd. That statement, not the imagery of the shepherd, had provoked the Jews to try to stone Jesus (John 10:31), for in their terms it was blasphemous (John 10:33). It was not something easily forgotten. Nor must we forget. If we seek God, we find him in the Son.

Another way of putting it is that Jesus is the Way into the Holiest spoken of in Hebrews 9:8 and 10:20. As Hebrews 10:19-25 says, we have boldness to approach the Holiest by the new and living way which Jesus has opened up for us, and is. But here also we hear the echoes of the blood of sacrifice for sin (Hebrews 10:19), for no one could safely enter the Holy Place except bearing blood to atone for sin (cf. Hebrews 9:7). Immediately, therefore, we are reminded of Jesus' words to the disciples in the Upper Room, 'No one comes to the Father except through me.'

The King James Version may put that better; 'no one comes to the Father but by me', for its last words bring together both the question of access and the selection of the believer, which is one of the deeper truths we have already encountered. Jesus is therefore both the Way to, and Access to, the Father. That brings to mind Jesus as the door or the gate of the sheep, which we looked at in Chapter 4, and brings in the notion of the door as defence and protection as well as access.

In many different senses Jesus is the Way of Salvation. The girl with the spirit of prediction who followed Paul and Silas in Philippi clearly understood that element. She cried 'These men are the servants of the Most High God, who are telling you the way to be saved' (Acts 16:17). Her demon (Acts 16:18) knew that Paul and his friends showed the Way of Salvation through preaching Christ and him crucified (1 Corinthians 2:2). But note also how the girl put it. It is the Most High God that was using Paul and the others to tell others the way to be saved. The girl was more accurate than my earlier sentence. Paul does not show the Way: God tells, through Paul and his friends.

In other terms this Way was also the Way of God into which the ebullient Apollos had to be educated by Aquila and Priscilla (Acts 18:26).

Jesus is also our leader on the Way. With him we are not on some infinite pilgrimage to which that silly saying applies: it is better to travel than to arrive. Those who travel in that frame of mind never get where they should be, and worse, on this journey run the risk of the fate of Ignorance which I described above. Aimlessness is not for us. We are on our way with our Master to the Father, and to where there are many mansions prepared for us (John 14:2).

And just to confuse matters in a wonderful conglomeration, it is also true that as soon as we start on the Way,

we have arrived. Those of us who can rejoice in the para-
doxes and pleasures of science fiction will get the most
pleasure here. You start from here to get to there, but you
never leave here throughout all the long way there, for the
Way is in us and we in him. Yet the Way is not an illusion.
We live in a moving present, and there is also movement
both in the spirit and in character. However, Jesus, the Way
and the Door is with us from the start. He is our starting
place, our route, transport, companionship, access to the
final destination, and that final destination all in one. Where
does that leave transmats, time tunnels, temporal loops and
hyperspace doors?

Jesus is also the Way of Truth, spoken of in 2 Peter 2:2,
and that takes us on to the second element of this 'I AM'
statement.

The Truth

'I am ... the truth.' What a deep saying that is. The scholars
tell us that in the Bible over half the uses of the related
Greek words which mean true, truth, genuine and reality,
are to be found in the writings of John. The beloved Apostle insists time and again that what he records is true, that
Jesus is reality, that his words are genuine. For him, 'I am
the truth,' struck deep, deep echoes, to the extent that some
have seen John as a gnostic writer, recording what he claims
to be a secret knowledge, a higher reality and deeper truth,
available only to the initiates, to the elite, to the chosen
few. But that is plain wrong. It is not true at all.

John's insistence is not that there is a higher reality, not
that there is a special truth for the most able and favoured
few, not that there is an arcane knowledge hidden from all
but the Masters and the Initiates. John claims the very re-
verse. He claims that the truth has come down to ordinary

mortals, that it is plain and open, that it has confronted Man and men, he and his friends, you and me. The first chapter of the Gospel of John makes that quite clear. So, if you found any pleasure in my comment at the start of Chapter 5 that in the latter three 'I AM' statements we are overhearing Jesus talking to his advanced class, beware. It is correct to put it that way, but this knowledge is offered to all. It is thus quite the contrary of gnosticism which is selective and secretive, where having folk outside the club is a primary point of the exercise, and where feelings of superiority are quietly massaged.

'I am ... truth.' What does that mean? Or do we ask Pilate's question, 'What is truth'? (John 18:38). Bacon says that jesting Pilate would not stay for an answer, but the ragged memory of Bacon's *Essay* ('Of Truth') gets in the way of the actual account. Pilate's question was evoked by Jesus' answer to a previous question, 'Are you the king of the Jews?' (John 18:33). Jesus ends his reply, 'Everyone who is on the side of truth listens to me' (John 18:37), and it is that sentence which triggers 'What is truth?'

We should note, however, that immediately Pilate had asked that question, and without waiting for a reply, he went out to the Jews and told them that he found no basis of charge against Jesus. Despite the tone of the question, which tradition has made cynical (but is it?), Pilate knew what Jesus meant. We, reading the accounts with open hearts, must acknowledge that we also know what Jesus meant. Either Jesus was mad, or he was and is who he said he was.

And if he is who he said he is, then what can be our question? He is reality. He is the truth about Man. He is the truth about you and the truth about me. For in him we see what we are not, and what we are. We see what sin has done in us, has done to us, and has done through us.

Jesus is also the truth about God. He is in the Father, and the Father is in him (John 14:10). Whoever has seen him has seen the Father (John 14:9). God is not remote, an absentee landlord, the clock-maker who has built the machine and gone off and left it. Nor is he a bloody, tyrannical figure, punishing viciously for minor infractions, and finding fault for what is his own fault. Nor is he an arbitrary sadist. Rather in Christ, the Redeemer, we see the God who would send his Son into the world to save the world (John 3:16-17). In his Son, God went to Calvary for us, not as a symbol or demonstration, but as a reality, taking our sin on his shoulders. The extraordinary words of Paul need to be swallowed, almost as a pill must, without analysis, so that they can do us good: 'God made him who had no sin to be sin for us, so that in him we might become the righteousness of God' (2 Corinthians 5:21). That is the fundamental meaning of 'I am ... the truth.'

The Life

There are many links for the last section, 'I am ... the life.' It suffuses many other of the 'I AM' statements. There is the Bread of Life, and the Resurrection and the Life. There is the Good Shepherd, whose sheep are alive and well under his care. There is the True Vine, which is obviously living. Even the Light of the World can provide some tinge to the notion of life, for living flame is different from luminescence, and light is essential for all life. In these ways, therefore, the other notions contribute and are brought into play. Yet in this 'I AM' there is another facet to concentrate on.

Here, where we are also being told of the Way to the Father and the Father's house, and where we are hearing of Truth, we are also confronting God, the source of all life, the creator, the sustainer and the nourisher. It is abundance of life which Jesus offers, the overflowing fecundity of Eden once more, not a mere existence. This is the God who is spoken of as El Shaddai ('Almighty God' in the King James Version), that Nourisher and Sustainer who promises children to the elderly Abraham in number as the sands of the sea, or as the stars of heaven (Genesis 13:1-3; 15:5-6; 17:1-2). He is the Nourisher, that Enricher, who speaks to that old age pensioner sitting in the gloaming outside his tent. It is that God who is to make Abraham fruitful at an age when children would not ordinarily be looked for, either from him or from Sarah. It is that Sustainer God to whom Job speaks, as he recognises his need of such a one. Does it surprise or comfort to know that the Book of Job has the largest number of references to this name of God? It is to El Shaddai, the Nourisher and the Sustainer, that Job cries. And then, in majestic transformation, it is Jehovah who answers him – God in his strength.

Therefore, when in John 14 Jesus speaks of himself as the life, he fills our horizons. He calls us to a fullness beyond expectation. We are not to become facile or shallowly 'joyful' about it, but neither are we to be lugubrious, and certainly we are not to become either inert or apathetic, glumly awaiting our call to 'higher things' in the future life. We are to rejoice with those that rejoice, and weep with those that weep (Romans 12:15). We are to be detached from everything but him (1 Corinthians 7:29-31). But, seeing his hand in creation, we are also to rejoice in its glories. There is glory to be found in a crystal, a waterfall, a mountain, the sea. There is even greater glory in living things, a sequoia, a flower, a blade of grass, a cactus, a bird, a cat.

These raise our attention to the highest form of life: Man, even you and me. Human life is the most marvellous thing

that has been created, that is, and that we shall ever encounter. That a few pints of water, a couple of nails' worth
of iron, a fair amount of carbon, a variable quantity of fat
and a whole host of minor elements, should stand on its
feet and contemplate the vastness of the cosmos is itself
amazing. That that same conglomeration should be made a
citizen of heaven (Ephesians 2:19) is marvellous beyond
words. But it is not marvellous to the point of insanity. It is
truth. We are not over-compensating for childhood depri-
vation, or fantasizing out our hurts, our inadequacies or
our disappointments. We are simply taking in the Bible's
message.

God is the Father and we know him in and through
Jesus, as he says again and again throughout John 14. The
result of that knowledge is love and life. As Jesus says, 'If
anyone loves me, he will obey my teaching. My Father will
love him, and we will come and make our home with him'
(John 14:33). 'Make our home with him' – there is the
nub. To live in such close fellowship with the Father and
the Son can seem daunting, but that is what it is all about.
And in any event it is not so strange, for they are with us
already. '... because I live, you also will live. On that day
you will realise that I am in my Father, and that you are in
me, and I am in you' (John 14:19-20).

Once again note that all this is not passive, although it
may make us more contemplative. We are not being in-
vaded by some parasite which will sap our vitality. Nor are
we being infected with some disease which will make us
hyperactive, until we expire of exhaustion. We are to live
normal, proper lives. There is life to be lived in him, enjoy-
ing and making the best use of whatever he sends us. Life
is conduct. That is clear from the words we have quoted.
Keeping his commandments and obeying his teaching are
the outworking of our love of him. In a sense they are but

by-products of that love, but they are necessary by-products as John makes clear in his epistles. Love of God must necessarily issue in love of one's fellows, and that can be hard at first. For some, indeed, all this may seem to work the other way around, starting as, 'These are the rules. Obey them. Love others.' But as we try to live according to these rules, we soon see the face of Jesus behind the rules, and the whole is swiftly turned the right way up.

And when that is done? When things are the right way up, we see that what at first seemed a strange, even an odd and disparate collection of images, is indeed a symphony in three movements. He is the way, the truth and the life.

CHAPTER 7

THE TRUE VINE

We are in John 15:1-11. Jesus is on his way to Gethse-mane. He has left the Upper Room where he and his disciples have recently celebrated Passover, and transformed that rite into the Lord's Supper. Only minutes before he has spoken of his being 'the way, the truth and the life'. Now as they hurry on, a different aspect of that life is to be made clear to the disciples.

Imagine them passing through the narrow, steep streets, down from the Upper City to the Valley Gate. It is dark as they go, dark but for the stars and the flare of a torch or two. The moon is hidden by ragged clouds. The fitful torch-light casts shadows, occasionally highlighting Jesus' face as he speaks hurriedly to them, he knowing that he goes to his betrayal, and, within hours, to his death. And yet, is there not humour in the words, a certain playfulness as he expands the analogy? Try saying his words aloud, as they are usually read in a church service. Then imagine them said as you walk down a steep cobbled road. There is a jerkiness about them which is conquerable only if a jocular element is brought out. The usual sonorous declamation of these words is misconceived. Judas has gone, and Jesus, relieved, is revelling in his last few minutes before dread events begin.

One of the fascinating things about 'I am the true vine' is its simplicity. Although Jesus is once more speaking only to his closest followers, there is an easily accessible level to what he says. This is not 'the resurrection and the life'.

Glorious though that was, it was difficult to penetrate. This is not 'the way, the truth and the life', a dense saying, too difficult for the disciples at first hearing. Its depths were to be plumbed only after much concentrated thought, and after the events of Calvary. Those codes were not easily broken.

'I am the true vine' is also a statement in code, but an easy code ... or is it? 'I am the true vine; you are the branches' (John 15:5) is clear enough, but the first thing Jesus says is, 'I am the true vine, and my Father is the gardener' (John 15:1), which is a different matter. That statement echoes back through the Old Testament. There was in history an untrue vine to contrast with Jesus' claim, and that vine had indeed been dealt with by its Gardener.

An Old Testament Theme

The idea of the vine plays a major part in Old Testament imagery. That woody creeper was an important asset, giving grapes, and if properly dealt with, wine. Despite its ragged appearance it was valued and cared for. Its cultivation was a specialised and a demanding art. In the first place cleaning an area of land in a stony place like Palestine was a lot of work. There would be the installation of drainage or more probably the putting in of an irrigation system. There would be a need to wall off the enclosure even before planting to keep out animals, and to protect the vines as they grew from the depredations of goats and others. Then the vine itself had to be cared for. The vine shoot is a tender thing, easily damaged by wind (another reason for the hedge or wall), and bruised by rough handling. As today, the vine had to be supported. In those days little poles or props were used to keep the vine off the ground, trellises being introduced only in Roman times.

Then diseases and pests had to be coped with. There were rules based on interpretations of Deuteronomy 22:9 as to the degree to which a vineyard could be used for growing other plants or weeds allowed, 'mixed seeds' being prohibited.[1] Any failure to observe these rules meant that the vineyard, and the wine, would be ceremonially unclean and could not possibly be used. In short, there was constant work involved keeping vines right and profitable, work both necessary for botanical and for theological reasons. And to cap all that, think of the heat!

The imagery of the Jews as the vine of God is found in various Old Testament passages. One example is Psalm 80, which starts by seeing God as the shepherd of Israel, therefore curiously tying together what we are to find here with the material of our Chapter 4. However, from verse 8 the imagery changes. The Psalmist is seeking restoration for the people (Psalm 80:3, 7, 14, 19). God had taken a vine from out of Egypt and cleared a place for it (verses 8-9). Under his care it had grown and spread (verses 10-11), but now he had broken down its protecting walls, allowing passers-by and wild beasts to help themselves to its grapes (verses 12-13). The vine was being cut down and burned (verse 16). Why? Because the Lord was punishing the people, although, as we shall see, the Psalmist was not entirely without hope (verses 17-19).

Ezekiel twice uses a similar figure. In Ezekiel 15 the Lord compares the people to a vine, speaking of it as a low creeping woody plant, useful for nothing but burning. Unfaithfulness had made the people fit for nothing but such a fate. Even though they had been through the fire once already, they had learned nothing from the experience (Ezekiel 15:7-8). In Ezekiel 17, what had been the cedar of

1. These rules are summarised in the Mishnah tractate *Kilaim*, see Danby, cited Appendix 1.

Lebanon has been cropped by the eagle of the Babylonians, and a noble shoot made a mere spreading vine. However, that vine had sought the help of another eagle. It could have borne fruit where it had been placed, but, because of its treachery, it has to be further cropped (Ezekiel 17:1-10). Verses 11-21 go on to translate the figure for Ezekiel's audience, to make sure that they get the point. The leaders of the Jews had been taken to Babylon, and yet, as soon as he had opportunity, the vassal king left in charge of those who remained in the land had gone to Egypt for help. The Jews left in the Land had not perceived punishment as the essential nature of what they were undergoing. Further punishment would therefore be inflicted. The Jews had neither kept their oath to the Babylonians, nor had they accepted the punishment sent by the Lord.

The picture of the people as a vine or the vineyard of the Lord is also taken up by Isaiah. There is pungent condemnation of the people in Isaiah 5. Psalm 80 was querulous as well as seeking comfort. In the Psalmist's words there is more than a trace of grievance; why has this happened to us? But in the Psalm there is also a sense that things will come all right eventually. Such notions get short shrift in Isaiah 5. As the Psalmist had seen, the Lord had taken his vine from Egypt and planted it in a fair land, removing stones from the ground and walling off an enclosure for the choicest vines. Yet the fruit of that vineyard was bad (Isaiah 5:1-4). The Lord would therefore remove the vineyard's protections, and the rain would cease to fall on it. The vineyard will become a wasteland, and thorns and briars will grow among the drought (Isaiah 5:5-6). Verse 7 translates the whole picture. Punishment is coming because the Lord had cared for the people, but they had turned to murder and oppression rather than justice and righteousness.

The message of the vine is the same through Isaiah and Ezekiel. The vine of Israel was not producing as it should have done, and that failure would have consequences. Even the writer of Psalm 80 saw something of what was to happen, though his optimism remains. And these examples are but the major instances of such imagery. When, therefore, Jesus spoke of himself as the true vine, there were clear examples in the Old Testament to provide the contrast of an untrue vine.

The Branch

But I am sure that by now some will be thinking, what about Jesus the Branch, and the promises about him? Indeed, it is time that we turned to these matters, for, in addition to those awful warnings, the Old Testament does provide details that part of the vine of Israel would breed true, and bear good fruit. Ezekiel 17, for example, ends with a promise that a further shoot of the cedar which had been cropped and made into a lowly vine, will be taken, and that it will grow into a mighty tree (Ezekiel 17:22-24). How was this to come about?

We can start with Psalm 80 once more, where, as a last thought before the refrain, the Psalmist writes, 'Watch over this vine, the root your right hand has planted, the son [or, 'the branch'] you have raised up for yourself .... Let your hand rest on the man at your right hand, the son of man you have raised up for yourself' (verses 14-15, 17).

Who can this 'son of man' be? Of course from our point in history, we know that this is Jesus, but that identification was not clear at the time the Psalmist wrote. He may have had some contemporary in mind, and have seen a chance of revival and faithfulness there (cf. verse 18). Other prophets, therefore, had to make the matter clearer. Of them,

Isaiah is the most pointed, and he uses the imagery of the vine to carry the message of promise, as well as the prophecy of judgement we have already looked at.

Some paragraphs back, I cited Isaiah 5 as a chapter where the people were condemned under the figures of a vine or vineyard. Their fruit was bad, hence they were to be grubbed up, their protective walls demolished, and the beasts allowed in. Such condemnation is also to be found in Isaiah 3, in the middle verses of which the Lord God takes his place in court and accuses the elders and leaders of the people of ruining his vineyard (Isaiah 3:13-14). (Incidentally we should perhaps note that for the judge to act as accuser was a common practice of the time. It is neither as odd nor as unjust as it may sound to one familiar with modern Anglo-American practice.) The Lord's indictment of the people, and his predictions of judgment carry right through the rest of the chapter and into the first verse of Isaiah 4. Then, suddenly, before the rigours of the vineyard imagery of chapter 5, there is an oasis of hope.

In that day the Branch of the LORD will be beautiful and glorious, and the fruit of the land will be the pride and glory of the survivors in Israel. Those who are left in Zion, who remain in Jerusalem, will be called holy, all who are recorded among the living in Jerusalem (Isaiah 4:2-3).

The whole of the rest of Isaiah 4 is worth reading, and, bearing in mind Chapter 3 of this book, I cannot forbear to point out verses 5 and 6, where the Lord says that there will be a cloud of smoke by day and a pillar of fire by night, with glory forming a canopy over all. This will be for a shelter and shade from the heat, and a refuge and hiding place from storm or rain. Once again, we find the resonances of another of the 'I AM' statements bound up with passages which inform us about others. In this case the light of the world is proximate to the Branch of the Lord, and the true vine.

Isaiah 4, therefore, contains this sudden oasis, sandwiched between the awful imagery of chapters 3 and 5. The coming of the Branch of the Lord, even in that dreadful day of punishment, provides a sudden promise of hope. But Isaiah has not done with such language and images. Isaiah 10 comes as a conclusion to another lengthy diatribe about the people and their shortcomings, with the bitter-sweet promise that at least the Lord will punish those who take it on themselves to punish the Jews. It is a bleak chapter. In the middle of it, however, there is a reference to what we moderns now call the doctrine of the remnant, the notion that the Lord will preserve some even in the coming desperations. Today we think of that as something fine, that the Lord's preservation of the remnant is his care for the people through whom Jesus would eventually come, and so it is. But those listening to Isaiah could only think of the saving of some while the most were to perish, as arbitrary, and as aggravating the horror for those who were to die. No. Our modern view is wrong. Isaiah 10 is gloomy and frightful, ending with the Lord laying into the thickets of the forest with an axe. Lebanon will be cut down, just as Ezekiel 15 and 17 had seen the dismemberment of the vine of Israel.

Then the prophet turns on another track. The axe will have done its work, and 'A shoot will come from the stump of Jesse; from his roots a Branch will bear fruit' (Isaiah 11:1). The rest of the chapter goes on to describe the day of that Branch in glowing terms. He will recall his people from wherever they have been scattered, and others, Gentiles, will also come:

In that day the Root of Jesse will stand as a banner for the peoples; the nations will rally to him, and his place of rest will be glorious. In that day the LORD will reach out his hand a second time to reclaim the remnant that is left of his people from Assyria, from Lower Egypt and Upper Egypt ... and from the islands of the sea (Isaiah 11:10-11).

We of the twentieth century, looking back, can see the shoot from the stump, which was to grow into a banner and was to recall his people, as the explanation of the preservation of the remnant of the Jews through all the holocaust of the Second World War, to say nothing of earlier pogroms, but its immediate reference was to preservation through the exile in Babylon, and through the havoc wreaked by other invaders. A faithful few would be preserved, from whom, and lineally from Jesse, the father of David, would come the man who could claim to be the true vine.

Others also saw something of all this. At one point, using the New International Version alternative version of Psalm 80:15 quoted above, I hoped that a case could be made for the identity of the 'son' and the 'branch' in that prayer, but apparently the uses of 'branch' to which we are coming can only mean branch or shoot, not son. Pity! But even without that, there is some fascinating material to be found.

We already looked at Jeremiah 23 in connection with the prophecies against the false shepherds (see Chapter 4). There Jeremiah begins with an indictment of the shepherds, and the promise of their replacement (Jeremiah 23:1-4). Then immediately the Lord speaks of raising from the line of David 'a righteous Branch, a King who will reign wisely and do what is just and right in the land. In his days Judah will be saved and Israel will live in safety. This is the name by which he will be called: The LORD Our Righteousness' (Jeremiah 23:5-6). Further on, Jeremiah speaks again of the restoration of the people, this time giving much detail about the recovery of the health of the land and its agriculture after the Babylonians had gone (Jeremiah 33:1-13). Then he repeats that the Lord will fulfil his gracious promises to the Jews, and 'will make a righteous Branch sprout from David's line' whose name will be 'The LORD Our Righteousness' (Jeremiah 33:15-16). In short, for those versed in Jeremiah, the idea of the Branch to come from that dry shoot of a vine was something to speculate about, and, from our point in time, that also casts a light in which to discern depths in the 'true vine'.

One other prophet uses such language, though the application of his imagery to Jesus is not so apparent. In Zechariah 3:8-10 the Lord announces to the high priest, Joshua, and his associates that he is going to bring his servant, the Branch. He then goes on to show them a seven-eyed stone, and to say that in one day he will remove the sin of the land, and then 'shall ye call every man his neighbour under the vine ...' That echoes through to our topic. Zechariah 4 then begins with the vision of the two olive trees and the seven branched candlestick, which we looked at in connection with the light of the world (see Chapter 3). Later in Zechariah 6 the prophet seeks to encourage Joshua by an acted parable. In some translations Joshua is the Branch who will branch out and build the temple of the Lord, though others will help (Zechariah 6:12-15). But fulfilment of that prophecy is all conditional upon obedience (Zechariah 6:15). History tells us that Joshua did not succeed. It was that other Branch, the one foreseen by Isaiah and Jeremiah, who did.

As all the Old Testament language and imagery (and not only that of the vine) approached a culmination and a fulfilment, we see therefore Jesus faithfully carrying out the task committed to him. The vine of the Jewish people had been planted in a good land, but had forfeited its privileges and therefore been pruned. Whole branches had been

cut down and thrown away. Much had been burned. Yet,
amid all that destruction a part of the vine still bred true,
and in due course from it would come right and proper
fruit. There were other tokens of that restoration. Such as
Simeon and Anna were praying faithfully in the Temple
and looking for the coming of Messiah. They were to see
him, and hold him (Luke 2: 25-32, 36-38). There was Elizabeth, and her husband Zechariah, from whom would come
the herald of the Lord (Luke 1:5-24, 39-44, 57-80). There
was Mary and Joseph, who were of David's line, though
one would look hard and long to see some trace of princely
status in their circumstances. Yet from that stump of Jesse,
the vine would once again blossom.

These pictures are clear, but there is one other which we
can also bear in mind as we think of that evening. As we
see Jesus hurrying to his betrayal, we are also seeing the
final episodes of the coming of the Son to claim his
Father's rights from those who had been entrusted with
the vineyard. As Jesus said when he used that figure, the
Son will be killed, and the Father would remove the wicked
tenants and give their job to others (Matthew 21:33-46;
Mark 12:1-12; Luke 20:9-19). How closely that parable
parallels the indictment of Isaiah 5:1-7, and how we have
seen it fulfilled as the Christian church has taken over the
role once entrusted to the Jews; but the question must be
asked, is today's church any more faithful to the owner of
the vineyard than were its predecessors as tenants?

The Branches

That question of faithfulness takes us across into the other
half of Jesus' statement. He is the vine. The corollary is
that first, the disciples, and secondarily, we, the other followers of Christ, are the branches of that vine. Fruit is re-

quired from these branches, and to that end the branches are subject to being pruned, like any normal well-cultivated vine is (John 15:2-7). The emphasis of the figure has therefore changed from the question of the vine's trueness, to that of its branches, their fruiting potential and the degree to which that potential is met. We are onto the rigours of cultivation.

Isaiah 5:1-2, and the parable of the wicked vine-dressers (Matthew 21:33-46; Mark 12:1-12; Luke 20:9-19), give us some idea of the work involved in establishing a vineyard and cultivating the vine. Recall what was said early in this chapter, cultivating the vine was hard labour. It required the clearing the ground of stones, installing drainage and walling off the enclosure, even before planting, to keep out animals. Then the vines had to be looked after. They had to be propped. The vineyard had to be constantly weeded to ensure that the prohibition against growing 'mixed seeds' of Deuteronomy 29 was not infringed. If it were, the whole vineyard might be rendered unclean. In short, Jesus saying that his Father was the Gardener tending his vine brings into play a whole panoply of associations which indicate the carefulness with which the Gardener carries out his exacting task of getting the best out of his vines. But the care goes beyond the environment of the vine, and can involve its pruning.

The Gardener cuts off every branch which does not bear fruit (John 15:2). We have already seen that simple point illustrated by the metaphor of the Jews as a vine. But there is an equally straightforward element to the point in the case of individuals. It is a matter of good husbandry. No fruit (or bad fruit) is precisely what makes any gardener take action. Anyone who has ever grown a fruit bush or tree which has failed to live up to expectations knows exactly what Jesus is talking about. If you plant for fruit, you want fruit, not mere decoration. There are decorative plants enough without allowing your vegetable patch to add itself to the herbaceous border. Certain trees apart (e.g. some varieties of cherry and almond), you do not grow a fruiting plant for its flowers alone. A lack of fruit is a call for the secateurs, if not for the spade.

But though what has just been written is true to what Jesus says, it could be depressing. It is therefore also important to recognise that the skill and knowledge of the gardener enters into his decision whether or not to prune. Think of it in domestic terms. My mother's garden had plum trees up at the back. For years one of them would produce a few misshapen plums, and its neighbour produced nothing. We thought of cutting them down, and were told that we should 'just wait'. In fact we kept them only because we used to sling a hammock between the two – a function hardly necessarily related to plums. Things continued like that for upwards of quarter of a century. Then, the first tree came into maturity. Now there are plums galore, for eating, jamming, freezing and bottling. And a couple of years after, its neighbour, the second tree, started to fruit and has done so each year subsequently, fruiting more and more heavily, producing lovely golden globes of sweetness.

Some fruit trees take longer than others to come into fruit, and some branches of Jesus' vine take longer than others. The thing to remember is that the Gardener knows what each should be doing. We should not rest complacent in the imagery of my analogy, but if we are doing as best we may, we should rely on the Gardener and not fear the knife. If, however, the failure to bear fruit is wilful, through intention or through sloth, we need to watch out. The Gardener of Jesus's vine knows, and deals with the branch which should be bearing but is not. That is the stark truth of John 15:2.

But the other half of John 15:2 has to be taken as well. The Gardener prunes the fruiting branches as well as the non-fruiting. That can seem unfair, as well as uncomfortable. Perhaps we can swallow the excision of the non-bearing branch, but what difference is there between it and the fruiting branch if that one also is pruned? The answer is again true to horticulture. Everyone knows that pruning, if properly done, encourages fruiting. Take out the old shoots and the new shoots will fruit as young wood, irrespective of the age of the plant. Fail to prune and the plant becomes coarse. It will make wood and not fruit, leaves and not flowers. In terms of Ezekiel 15, the resultant woody plant will be fit only for burning.

Further, the treatment of the fruiting branch is only superficially the same as the branch which is cut out, for the fruiting branch is not cut off. It is only pruned, but pruned constructively. No growing process is painless, and it is better to be the best that one can be, even at the expense of a little pruning. The New International Version makes all this clear in its translation of John 15:2, where it speaks of cleaning the branch to make it more fruitful. For myself, I again think of this in terms of memories.

When I was a child, our next-door neighbour, Mr Caie, had a vine in his greenhouse. It was an object of great interest, a vine in such a cold place as Aberdeen! And occasionally I was allowed in to see this exotic specimen. Every year I would see a dry, tattered, peeling stump, and each year that stump would send out new shoots, exactly as Isaiah saw the Root of Jesse sprouting. Those shoots would send out shoots, and these shoots would send out yet more shoots. Old Caie-Caie had a very sharp thin-bladed knife, and with it he trimmed off most of these subsidiary side-shoots to encourage the initial shoots to grow strongly so they would later produce good bunches of grapes from well set up trusses. He also pruned to prevent a matting of the weak sub-shoots where the white-fly and fungi could lurk. And in his pruning he was very, very careful, because vine shoots are tender and 'bleed' if not correctly dealt with. Careless pruning damages the entire vine, wasting its substance. Careful pruning works wonders. Clean cuts, well-executed, are essential.

That is exactly what Jesus says God does with each of us. We are branches and need careful cleaning. We will be pruned to get the best fruiting out of us, so we grow strong and not flaccid, and so as to prevent spindly weak over-crowded branchlets where fungus and beasties can create damaging infestation. We are dealt with by a master of the gardening craft.

And what is our fruit? In this imagery it is not 'souls for Christ': that comes with other figures of speech. Within the imagery of the vine and the branches, souls are other branches. The end result of the fruit of the vine may indeed be other branches springing from the main root of the vine, but 'the fruit of the Spirit is love, joy, peace, patience, kind-ness, goodness, faithfulness, gentleness and self control. Against such things there is no law' (Galatians 5:22-23). These are the grapes of the branches of the vine; from them is the wine of the Spirit.

But in order to bear fruit a branch must have the life of the vine passing into and through it. The sap must run, nourishing it and making it live. Accordingly, Jesus talks of the necessity of remaining in the vine (John 15:4-6). There is a reciprocity also in these verses: we remain in him and he remains in us – the result is fruit. Such 're-maining' is different from the Gardener pruning or not pruning, and it brings into our thinking on these matters the element of choice. God's cutting off of an unfruitful branch confirms the unfruitfulness of that branch, but that unfruitfulness is voluntary on the part of the branch. What it has chosen to be, God states that it will be forever, for fruitfulness depends on the life of Jesus flowing through the individual.

The life of Jesus in each of us is not only something precious, it is fundamental. This point is on the periphery of other of the 'I AMs', but it is brought to the forefront of our thinking by Jesus' exposition of it here. Why it should be brought out plainly now in Jesus' ministry, and not earlier, is a question. The reason may be that the traitor Judas had gone. Jesus could not have spoken of him as being a branch of the true vine. Now, however, Jesus is with his branches, those who are true and who have his life in them. Now he can speak of that integration and essential essence of life in him in relatively plain terms, and in the knowledge that he is speaking of all his audience.

We often talk of 'the Christian life.' It is a neat phrase, but it is misleading, for it contains a transferred epithet. In its usual form the phrase seems to imply that the Christian life is a role into which you slip as and when needed, much as if you had come on stage. But we are living Christians, not persons who (occasionally) live a Christian life. For a Christian, living involves Jesus just as much as it does heart, blood, nerves, muscles and fat. Jesus is not something external, the pattern of a role which we play. Nor is he a life-support system, an external, mechanical help for a body which cannot cope on its own. As branches of the living vine, we are not plugged into a mass of tubes, pistons, cogs and motors which somehow makes us live as Christians. We do not lie on a hospital bed in sterile surroundings, ultimately dependent on an electric switch. We stride down the street, run across the dunes, yomp across moor and hill. We, and he, together.

We are branches of the true vine, integral parts of the

whole, and natural parts of it. Jesus speaks in those terms. Elsewhere Paul writes of grafting, but he then talks of grafting of olives, and not of vines (Romans 15:16-21). (Sometimes the delicate meshing of Scripture is astonishing.) Paul makes the point that we are grafts and on that account should be the more careful because our entitlement to our position is less certain than that of the original branches. It is a fair warning, but it is not what Jesus is saying in John 15. He is the vine, and his followers are the branches. They are held up to the light, and nourished from the root, so that fruit may result. We grow from his root and stem as part of his life. Our life in him is not an implant into us, nor is his life in us an implant into him. We are new men and women. It is not our old natures which have been grafted onto his root, but rather we grow from him new. The imagery is not exact but the point is there.

The point is there, and we need to make it, for there is something else which needs to be looked at carefully. The branches which are cut off wither and are burned (John 15:6), and that is something which can worry certain sensitive souls. Removed from the vine, the branch dies. Does this mean that one can fall away into utter destruction even after one has been Christ's? I do not think so. There are too many other places in the Bible, some of them among the 'I AM' statements, in which Jesus speaks of his holding on to those that are his, and that they do not fall out of his hand. It is found, for example, in the conversations surrounding the shepherd imagery (Chapter 4), and in the context of the way, the truth and the life (Chapter 6). Jesus also clearly speaks of this in his prayer in Gethsemane (John 17). His imagery in John 15 speaks of fruit and the consequence of lack of fruit. It does not say that a branch of the vine becomes anything other than a branch of the vine, even if the branch is cut off and burned. That, of course, is

desperately serious for the branch, but it is not utter condemnation. Such a soul is, in Paul's words, 'saved, but only
as one escaping through the flames' (1 Corinthians 3:15).

But this is too gloomy. Look rather at the other side.
Look at the branches which bear fruit. It is true that they
will be pruned, and that will be a sore experience, no doubt.
But the purpose is yet more fruit. God seeks fruitfulness in
each of us.

In that connection we should each bear in mind that what
God considers fruit in our case may be very different from
what we might think. And different from what others might
expect, and even demand. We need to remember that God
considers us each as individuals in this, as in all other matters. We are not in competition with each other, nor are we
compared in his eyes. The stronger branch need not, and
should not, feel superior to the less strong. Measured against
its potential the strong branch may be doing quite poorly,
while the apparently weak branch may be fruiting beyond
expectation, although we see very little. But, if we have
assimilated the teaching of this 'I AM' as well as the others, that is a point which need be only stated, not under-
lined.

Now, do you see what has happened? We have turned
from talking about Jesus to talking about ourselves and
each other. That is one marvellous thing about this, the
final 'I AM.' It brings us through to an awareness of each
other, and of Jesus in each other. We see him in our neighbour, and even in ourselves. Think of your Christian friends,
and think of yourself. Try, if you will, to think of what he
or she might have been like but for the sap of the Jesus-
vine running through. Then do the same for yourself, which
may be an easier task, for you know yourself better. This 'I
AM' sees Jesus and the individual brought very close together, closer even than the shepherd/sheep images. It

brings individuals close together also as branches of the single vine. We should be more tolerant of others, and less tolerant of our own shortcomings. We should be more helpful both to others, and to ourselves, in our effort to produce many large bunches of good grapes.

And yet even that image is wrong, for there is no effort in a vine fruiting. It just does it. How is your foliage? How are your flowers? What about the bugs, the frost, and the weakening, small side-shoots? Are you fruiting well, and carrying your grapes to a ripe maturity?

For some, however, there are difficulties with such imagery, for they, for the best of reasons, find the ideas of the vine and the grape off-putting. The association of the vine with wine, and of wine with alcohol abuse, can diminish the pleasure and the teaching which others can derive from the imagery. If that is the case, then remember that for the Israelites, and for the Jews of Jesus' day, wine was crucial. In a hot climate, without a clean water supply, wine was the only general drink which it was half-way safe to drink. Only a few would take the Nazarite vow to refrain from wine (Numbers 6:3), or the Rechabite vow which had a similar clause (Jeremiah 35:6-7). John the Baptist abstained from wine (Luke 1:15), while Jesus was accused of being a drunk (Matthew 11:18), and changed the water into wine at the wedding in Cana (John 2:1-11).

It was precisely because only wine was a safe drink that some vines were fit only for burning. The vine which fruited inadequately, or which gave bad grapes was worse than useless, using up time and effort on the part of its gardeners, and also using ground which could have produced a more useful crop. Promising sustenance and a degree of pleasure, such a vine does not deliver. It provides no recompense for toil. Bad grapes and bad wine are in themselves abominable. Measure thus the degree of God's disillusionment with the vineyard he had planted, and given to the leaders of the people to tend. A bad grape or a mouthful of bad wine is not something which one deals gently with.

On the other hand a good vine, a true vine, gives quality grapes in abundance. It massively repays the work and care which has been lavished on it. I think of a vine in a garden in Hungary, stretching on its trellis across the whole of the breadth and half the length of the garden, providing shade for the whole family, and festooned with toothsome grapes. Think of the spies sent in to Canaan by the people. They came back with a bunch of grapes which it took two of them to carry, slung on a pole between them (Numbers 13:23). See there the promise of the true vine, and through him, the promise of the fruitfulness of his carefully and well-pruned branches.

Apart from our Lord we can do nothing (John 15:5). If we remain in him, he will remain in us (John 15:8). The result will be much fruit, to the glory of God the Father (John 15:8). That is what the Lord God, the Gardener of the True Vine, the planter of Eden, desires.

CHAPTER 8

BREAD TO VINE

The first chapter of this book told of the sequence of paintings by Monet of the West Front of the Cathedral at Rouen,
and of the other sequence of the haystack in the field. Each
sequence was done from the same vantage-point, but at
different hours of the day and of the year. Passing from
one picture to another along the sequence enlightens. One
comes to know the subject in a way not possible if you
only consider each picture in isolation.

There is another way to think of Jesus' word-pictures.
Nowadays, remote sensing satellites scrutinise the earth
through different filters and at different wave-lengths. The
images are relayed back to earth and analysed, compared
and consolidated. Each image can be coded to bring out
different information. Contrasts between pine trees and,
say, oak can be highlighted by instructing the computer to
show the green of oak leaves as blue and that from pine as
red. Grass land can be displayed as one colour and wheat
another. In this way the images bring out something different about vegetation and ground-cover. Analysed they
can tell us much about the countryside, about heat distribution on land, and in river and sea, about the underlying
geology of an area, about weather patterns. Different filters and different wave-lengths permit all sorts of information to be discovered about the surface of the earth, and
many useful deductions to be made. But in order to do

that, the satellite pictures are not whole and complete in themselves. They concentrate on some matters and leave others entirely obscure. The familiar shots on the television weather forecast are built up from many pictures which concentrate on one thing rather than another.

In a sense Jesus' 'I AM' statements are remote sensing imagery, colour coded to bring out clearly one set of particular information rather than another.

In both instances, the Monets or the satellite imagery, the individual pictures can inform, but the comparison of pictures can bring out more. While you can superimpose satellite photographs to vary the information from them, or use a separation technique to produce a 'three-dimensional' picture, you cannot do the same with the Monets. Nonetheless, it is now time to attempt something similar with Jesus' 'I AM' statements. In each of them he highlights different facets of himself, aspects of his nature, his personality and his work, who he was and what he had come to do. We can also gather data from the reactions of his audiences to what he said.

In one way, therefore, we do seek to superimpose Jesus' word-pictures. We must seek to hold each image in tension with the others, and with such other data as we have in the Bible so that we do not allow a favourite image too much prominence. That is difficult, for we each have our own preferences; I find the image of the good shepherd very appealing. It goes back to some of my earliest Christian teaching from my mother. But we must keep a balance between the images so as to see exactly what Jesus was saying about himself, and to feel how that affects us. It is better to understand and appreciate what he says than to produce our own ideas about him. It is better to deal with reality, and not some invention of our own – that way there is less likelihood of a nasty shock on some future occasion!

But in another sense, of course, we simply cannot superimpose the images at all. What we have done in the
previous chapters is like walking from picture to picture in
Boston Art Gallery. Now we are to stand back and let our
eyes flit along the line from a distance. The time for close-
up detail is past. We now know enough to translate the code
of each picture. We have considered the features of each
individually, and can now pass quickly from element to
element. Given the detail of the previous chapters, a mere
reference to a component should be enough to bring it to
mind and into focus, when we need it. Perhaps also the
speedy passing from one element to another, from one picture to another, will blend them together, much as one uses
a sequence of still photographs to produce 'moving pictures.'

First, however, let's see what we can get from the reactions of the audiences, and from the way in which he deals
with them.

The first thing to observe is Jesus' treatment of his audience. He is patient with the crowd which sought bread,
though he tried to lead them to profounder matters, and in
measure they were willing to be so led. At first, in fact,
they make the running, but, after he has made the message
just the slightest bit plainer, many back off. In the 'light of
the world' passages the warning of the alternative to choosing the light is more definite, and less allowance is made
for the foibles of the crowd. The message about 'the good
shepherd' and the sheep makes no concessions and is a
scathing attack on the arrogance and wilful conduct of the
Pharisees, who should have cared for the man born blind.

But these were occasions of a mass audience. As one
would expect, when with his own folk Jesus tailors his treatment to the individual need. With Martha he is gentle and
humorous as he leads her to think of him as 'the resurrec-

tion and the life'. With the disciples he is both deliberately 'difficult', and teasing, as he draws them into the deeper waters of 'the way, the truth and the life'. There is the extended humour of the 'true vine' and its branches, which can be taken in part as a joke shared with his friends.

But, underlying these different ways of dealing with each audience, there is the urgency of what Jesus has to say. Urgency and importance come clearly through in the first four 'I AM' statements. Jesus makes it very plain that what he has to say is vitally important, and that there is need of haste in accepting it. In the 'bread of life' and the 'light of the world' he states and re-states in plain if picture language, who he is and what he has come to do. He has come down from the Father in heaven to be bread, providing a permanent nourishment and also restoring relations with the Father. He is a sacrifice and a reminder and evidence of God's love. He is light for the world, both in warning and in guidance. He is the light of illumination, and protection, a beacon of warning and of safety. He is the good shepherd, who cares for his flock and gives his life for it. He is the door to the sheep-fold for them.

In the 'good shepherd' and the 'door' imagery particularly, Jesus also makes clear that there is a special flock which he is gathering and protecting. Those who belong to him hear his voice and follow him. He is their safety and security. That is, perhaps, the side of that passage which we grasp to ourselves. There is another side, however, and it is one which we dare not forget. In the 'good shepherd' Jesus both by implication, and by express statement, shows his deep anger with the false shepherds, false because they have neglected their calling. Those who should have served the flock, even to the sacrifice of their own lives, had instead sought to domineer. Their contempt for the simple honesty of the man born blind rouses divine anger, and, drawing deeply on terrifying analogues from the Old Testament, Jesus laid into them. The contrast with his tender seeking out of the man later, and revealing himself to him as the Son of Man, is striking in itself (John 9:35-38). It is the more striking to recognise that this was the Saviour of the world seeking out an individual member of his flock, just as a good shepherd does (cf. Luke 11:1-7).

Then there is that profound change as Jesus no longer speaks to the crowds, and to the scribes, the Pharisees and the Sadducees, but talks with and to friends and disciples. From emphasising the urgent need to recognise and accept him, he then begins to reveal the wonders of life with him. The earlier 'I AM' statements did speak of nourishment, protection, life and the like, but these matters are made more explicit as the imagery becomes more personal, and is revealed more on a direct basis to chosen individuals. Jesus is no longer speaking to a large group, many of whom were hostile, but to those whom he knows, to his sheep. With tender skill he draws from Martha her recognition of him as the 'resurrection and the life,' and, once Judas Iscariot has gone on his fateful errand, he tells the disciples of the 'way, the truth and the life'. Finally, and with teasing good humour, he speaks of that simplest of images, the 'true vine' and its 'branches' as he goes to the first scene of the last act of his earthly ministry. In these later images he thus provides for his friends metaphors and analogies which were to yield their fuller meaning only after they had been long chewed over in the light of his ministry and Calvary itself. These ways of thinking of him and his life were to help them really grasp what had been done and who he was. We, reading them, can do so also, and if we do so grasp, they allow us also to pass through the images to friendship with him.

Of course, as we have seen, the images Jesus used trans-

mit a meaning not only in their immediate aspect. The superficial element of the word picture was but part of what
it contained. Each has roots and resonances within the Old
Testament which fill out and add to the richness of what
was being said. These allow us, and did allow Jesus' audience, to decipher the code which each image presents as it
echoes and resonates back into revelation. Often Jesus indicates that his audience was blind in not seeing the connection between his words and their Old Testament precedents. He also found fault with them in not using those
precedents to decode his message. The scribes and the
Pharisees were especially without excuse. These students
of the Scriptures should have been able to follow his referents, for they were accustomed to the 'leaping logic' of
which we wrote in Chapter 1. But they did not. They were
wilfully blind. Trapped in the intricate choreography of their
theology, most of them would not acknowledge that Messiah had come, although blessedly there were some of his
sheep among them (cf. John 10:21, 41-42; 11:45; 12:11).
They would not, for example, make any connection between Micah 5:2-5 and the man speaking to them, even if
he spoke of true shepherding and had been born in Bethlehem.

No: on the contrary, there is an ominous progression in
the attitude of the scribes and the Pharisees. The 'bread'
discussion seems to intrigue many of them, and some come
close to the truth before sheering away from it. At the 'good
shepherd' discourse they are shown to be more interested
in parsing their theological and legal niceties than caring
for one who should have been their concern, and whose
being healed should have gladdened their hearts. By the
time of the resuscitation of Lazarus they had had enough
and are out to kill Jesus. Previously they had sought to
execute Jesus for blasphemy, but that was in the heat of the

occasion (e.g. John 8:58-59). Now there is a cold-blooded planning and scheming. 'It is expedient for us that one man should die for the people, and that the whole nation perish not' (John 11:50, KJV) is *realpolitik* at work. But to add Lazarus to the death list, because people believed in Jesus because of his resuscitation, was villainous (John 12:10-11). It shows that more than politics was involved. There is a settled hatred there which goes beyond a mere rejection of Jesus' message and shows the roots of that rejection to lie with God's Enemy. In other words, I suspect this shows that the Old Testament roots of Jesus' images were, in fact, well recognised by those they were directed at. Are not their actions understandable only on the assumption that the rejecters were maddened by a fear that Jesus' warnings and his claims were accurate and true?

I ask that question because another characteristic of Jesus' sayings is that, where they are testable, they are accurate. He is often elliptic in what he says. He never tells all, and often his audience, and even the disciples, misunderstand. He tells the Jews and later the disciples that he is going where they cannot follow him (John 7:34; 8:21; 13:33). He tells the Jews and the disciples that they will then search for him and not find him (John 7:34-36; 13:33). He tells the disciples that Lazarus's sickness will not end in death (John 11:4), without telling them that Lazarus will go through death and be raised again (cf. John 11:23).

To me, these and the other instances of Jesus' accuracy add immeasurably to the urgency of his statements; choose, follow, eat ... Even without the Old Testament resonances of the images, what he is saying comes through again and again, and always with the overtone of the need for haste. Add the connections of the Old Testament and an inexorable magnificence becomes apparent. One is free to choose, and yet there is a pattern; what in *Perelandra* C. S. Lewis called The Great Dance. The sheep know his voice.

Is that the explanation why some grasp and act on the message of these images, and others do not? It does not seem to have much to do with intellectual ability or discernment, for even the disciples did not always immediately comprehend what was being said. Of course they may have the excuse of not being educated men, but sometimes Jesus is impatient with them; or is it that he tries to stimulate them by his comments (e.g. John 14:9)? Be that as it may, he did also promise that later they would understand, and that they would remember his words as and when they needed to (John 14:17, 26; 16:13; Luke 24:15). We are the beneficiaries of the keeping of that promise.

There is, however, another explanation of why such as the disciples responded and others did not, and it brings us close to what for many is a deep and forbidding truth. We have seen that Jesus' 'I AM' sayings are, as it were, in code, and that code could be broken by use of 'leaping logic' to draw on its Old Testament origins. We have also seen how on occasion it seems that the scribes and the Pharisees did indeed follow that logic, but then rejected the conclusion to which they were thereby pointed. That process therefore parallels the reply of Jesus when the disciples asked him about the parables. Jesus had given them a clear statement of what he meant by certain parables, and they were puzzled. Why did he not give others that same knowledge? He replies that the disciples had been given the secret, but for the outsiders the message was to remain opaque so that 'though seeing, they may not see; though hearing, they may not understand' (Matthew 13:10-15; Mark 4:10-12; Luke 8:9-10; Isaiah 6:9-10. Cf. John 12:36-40, quoting Isaiah 53:1; 6:10). Jesus does not meet all the objections which are put to him: he explains only to a few. Otherwise he can be enigmatic and elliptic, while simultaneously being urgent and relentless. This is a great puzzle, and all we can do, in the knowledge of his testable accuracy, is to accept his word that his own sheep hear his voice and follow him (John 10:3-5, 27-29; cf. John 10:6, 26).

What do the pictures then leave us with? Is Jesus, as some would say, only a kindly, humorous and remarkable teacher, sometimes enigmatic in conversation, but always capable of presenting the duty to love one another in striking language? Or is he just another ancient whose message has survived the accidents of history, like those of Lao Tse, Confucius or the Buddha?

He is much more than these. He *is* kindly, humorous and caring. He *is* a remarkable teacher. But his message, repeated again and again through the different pictures of the 'I AMs', and elsewhere in other language, is far more compelling and urgent than that of the sages. He is the Son of God, sent from heaven to seek and to save the lost, to find and to rescue those whom the Father has given him. He is the bread of heaven given for nourishment. He is the light of the world. He is the good shepherd, and the door of the sheep-fold. He is the resurrection and the life. He is the way, the truth and the life. He is the true vine, that new shoot sprung from the tattered stump of the chosen people through whom salvation was to come. Through his branches he will bear good and abundant fruit. He is light, life, truth. He is sustenance, and the way. We must be integrated with him and into his life.

Ranging the gamut of these word pictures, we therefore have much to think about. Jesus has shown different facets of himself, and indicated different aspects of his work to different audiences. It is a masterly performance. But the one thing we must not do is to view it only as a performance. We are not watching a play. There is no interval here, no commercial breaks, no curtain calls, no 'real life' to which we return once the show is over. Jesus speaks to us, to each of us, as clearly as he spoke to the crowds and to his friends those centuries ago, confronting us with the same message, the same urgent need to choose, and the same result of choice. For us also he is the bread, the vine and all the intervening pictures.

So, finally, we can see one thing which draws all these pictures together. The images progress from bread to wine. There is a parabola here which is rooted in the bread and the wine of communion: 'This is my body... This is my blood' (Matthew 26:26-28; Mark 14:22-24; Luke 22:14-19). These elements were present in the very first of the 'I AM' episodes (cf. John 6:53-56), and they are transformed into the living union of the vine and the branches in John 15:1-5. 'Whoever eats my flesh and drinks my blood remains in me, and I in him' (John 6:56), is paralleled by, 'Remain in me and I will remain in you' (John 15:4).

We are sustained by, and only by, him. His broken body is our salvation. This is not a simple rescue where the rescuer is thanked, and the rescued goes off on his own business once again. This is salvation into a new relationship. We, saved, are forever fused into the life of the Saviour. Communion celebrates his act, and our continuing relationship with him.

That relationship comes through again and again in the pictures that we have been considering. The bread is food. The light is guidance and warning. The shepherd cares for his sheep and protects them both as shepherd and as door. He leads his flock to pasture. In him is resurrection and life. He is the way through life, through and on into the Holiest. He is the true path, and the truth about God and ourselves. He is the vine which sustains us, holding us up to the light and nourishing us from his well-set root.

But it is not a passive relationship we enter upon with

him. Through him we bear fruit, as much fruit as the branch will bear if we will permit that, and we are pruned so as to bear more and more, more in quantity and more in quality.

This is my body, which is for you ...
This cup is the new covenant in my blood (1 Corinthians 11:24-25).

APPENDIX 1

The Problem of Time: Sources

Some Bible words and expressions bring with them clear indications that they need to be thought about. The various instructions about sacrifices, for example, are not run-of-the-mill in modern practice, and you know that their meaning needs further explanation and exploration. When you come across words that are familiar you tend to assume that they mean what you understand by them in their normal modern use.

But there are times when that approach can mislead. As an academic lawyer, it is curious, for example, to read discussions of the Trial of Jesus, where modern authors both criticise what is done, and seek to draw lessons, on the basis of present day criminal procedure or the requirements of contemporary administrative law. On the contrary, one has first to see how these events might be construed by their contemporaries. And this is accentuated when reading the Epistles or Jesus' teaching in the Gospels. One must seek to know what the expressions used meant to their users, readers and hearers at the time, before constructing or deducing their meaning for modern purposes.[1] What was the importance of 'bread' or 'wine' in New Testament

---

1. I have discussed this at greater length in my *Slaves, Citizens, Sons: Legal Metaphors in the Epistles,* (Academie Press, Zondervan Publishing House, Grand Rapids, Michigan, USA, 1984), 'Of Metaphors and Analogies' 183-89, and in 'Of Metaphors and Analogies: Legal Language and Covenant Theology' (1979) 32 Scottish Journal of Theology, 1-17.

times? How did a shepherd then operate? And so on.

In the chapters of this book I have sought to make the best use I can of Bible dictionaries and encyclopedias to understand the world of Jesus' day. I have been quite catholic in my use of such sourcing, ranging across the standard dictionaries and encyclopedias irrespective of their denominational and theological orientation. As to books I have found helpful, Roland de Vaux's *Ancient Israel: Its Life and Institutions*, 2nd edn. (trans. J. McHugh, London: Darton, Longman Todd; New York: McGraw Hill Book Co., 1965). The writings of J. D. M. Derrett have been particularly stimulating for a lawyer. Of them, his *Jesus's Audience* (London: Darton, Longman and Todd, 1973), is a fascinating work. Various of his articles are available in his *Law in the New Testament* (London: Darton, Longman and Todd, 1970), and the (so far) five volume collection of articles, *Studies in the New Testament* (Leiden: E. J. Brill, 1977-89). They are also thought-provoking, making many links and establishing intriguing resonances.

APPENDIX 2

Leaping Logic

Just as it is necessary to attempt to understand biblical language in the concepts and resonances of their time, so one should seek to use the kind of thought processes that were then common. The way in which we accept the linking of ideas affects how and what we think. It was the same in biblical times. We can miss the point of what is said because we fail to recognise a link or perceive a linkage as unacceptable. The 'leaping logic' of biblical times was normal. As explained in Chapter 1, it could result in ideas being connected through puns, inversions, verbal similarities and mnemonic tricks. Such elements can be obscured in English and other translations.

The point is not confined to biblical studies. Herbert Danby, the translator of *The Mishnah*, (Oxford: Oxford University Press, 1933), considers the matter at pp. xxiii-xxvii. J. D. M. Derrett, whose books are noted in Appendix 1, has done much to show unexpected but convincing parallels and connections between different parts of the biblical text which depend on such leaping logic.

Scripture Index

100:3 72, 86
119:101, 104, 105 119

33:15-16 137
35:6-7 146

Ecclesiastes
12:3 25

Isaiah
3:13-14 134
4:2-3 134
5:1-2 139
5:1-4 132
5:1-7 138
5:5-6 132
6:1 61
6:10 156
6:9-10 156
9:2 52, 54
9: 6 52
10 135
11:1 135
11:10-11 136
20:11 72
26:19 103
38:17 103
40:3 118
40:11 86
43:14 117
43:16 117
44:28 74
53:1 156

Jeremiah
3:15 73
13:17 72
23:1-4 136
23:1-40 75
23:4 73
23:5-6 73, 136
25:10 25
33:1-13 137

Ezekiel
1:4 61
1:15-25 61
1:27-28 61
15:7-8 131
17:1-10 132
17:22-24 133
34:12 88
34:23 73
34:31 73, 75, 86
37:24 73
37 103
41:21-2 41

Daniel
7:9 60
12:2 102

Hosea
6:1-3 103
13:14 103

Micah
5:2-5 154
7:14 73

Zechariah
3:8-10 137
4 137
4:1-14 60
6:12-15 137
10:3 73, 86
11:12-13 75
13:7 76

Romans
4:1-25 27
12:15 125
13:11-13 64
15:16-21 144

1 Corinthians
2:2 121
3:11-13 65
3:15 145
7:29-31 125
11:24-25 159

2 Corinthians
3:13 61
5:21 124
11:14 62

Galatians
5:12 15
5:22-23 142

Ephesians
2:19 126

Colossians
1:12-13 63
2:2-3 40
3:1-4 40

1 Thessalonians
5:5-10 63

Hebrews
9:3-5 38, 40
9:7 120
9:8 81, 120
10:19-25 120
10:20 81

1 Peter
2:5 42
2:9 42, 63

2 Peter
2:2 122
5:1-4 87

1 John
1:5-7 66

2 John
1 110

3 John
1 110

Revelation
1:6 42
2:17 39, 40
5:10 42
18:22 25
20:6 42